Stay Golden!

GOLD IS A
BETTER WAY

GOLD IS A BETTER WAY

...And *Other* Wealth

Building Secrets

Wall Street

Doesn't Want You To Know

Adam Baratta

NEW YORK

LONDON • NASHVILLE • MELBOURNE • VANCOUVER

Gold is a Better Way

And Other Wealth Building Secrets Wall Street
Doesn't Want You to Know

Published in New York, New York, by Morgan James Publishing. Morgan James is a trademark of
Morgan James, LLC. www.MorganJamesPublishing.com

The Morgan James Speakers Group can bring authors to your live event. For more information or to
book an event visit The Morgan James Speakers Group at
www.TheMorganJamesSpeakersGroup.com.

ISBN 9781642791051 paperback
ISBN 9781642791068 case laminate
ISBN 9781642791075 eBook
Library of Congress Control Number: 2018945365

Cover Design by: Ray Griggs

Interior Design by: Ryan James Gonzales

Edited by: Charlotte Baratta

In an effort to support local communities, raise awareness and funds, Morgan James Publishing
donates a percentage of all book sales for the life of each book to Habitat for Humanity Peninsula
and Greater Williamsburg.

Get involved today! Visit www.MorganJamesBuilds.com

The **OUR HOUSE Grief Support Center** mission is to provide the community with grief
support services, education, resources, and hope. Since 1993, OUR HOUSE has helped
thousands of children, teens, and adults grieving the death of someone close.

Sharing Grief. Finding Hope.

To learn more, please visit

www.OurHouse-Grief.org or call **(888) 417-1444**

Published in Association with Brentwood Research Publishing,
a trademark of Brentwood Research, LLC
www.brentwoodresearch.com

In Loving Memory

For Buddy. Who loved with all of his being.
You will forever live inside our hearts.

*

Special Thanks

Relationships in Life are the real gold.

To Billy The Lion, keep roaring!
To everyone who supported me when life threw unhittable curveballs.
To Kirill and Josh, the best business partners
I could have ever hoped for.
And to Charlotte, who makes life worth living.

CONGRATULATIONS!

Redeem Your Special Gift

Worth Over $195!

(FREE for the First 10,000 People
Who Purchased a Copy of This Book)

It's Time to Take Control of Your Financial Future!

CONTENTS

Gold Price

$1,296

10 Year Treasury

2.40%

Dow Jones

24,824

INTRODUCTION

"The definition of insanity is doing the same thing
over and over again and expecting a different result"

Albert Einstein

Perhaps you have opened this book with a fair amount of skepticism. I hope so. The title *Gold Is A Better Way* was chosen specifically to have this impact. I hope you will read this book and challenge everything in it. As you do, please evaluate the logic and find as much fault with it as you can. This is where I began my own journey five years ago.

I believe that information is power. The information in this book is so powerful, you may be upset that nobody shared it with you before now. It's information that Wall Street definitely will not tell you. I want it to get you fired up and upset. Information learned without emotion is not retained. It's emotion that caused me to write this book and emotion that will get you to take action. Action that I believe is more necessary now than at any time in history.

As a companion to this book, I've spent over a year building and creating **goldisabetterway.com**, an educational member website where you can do your own comparisons, execute your own calculations, and find answers on your own. There are dozens of videos and additional content that will provide you tools to evaluate the markets like a professional. From there you can

1

develop a strategy. People pay thousands of dollars to get access to this kind of information. Because you have taken action and purchased my book, I am giving you access to this information for free. I believe you'll find it the most comprehensive site of it's kind ever created. The book and companion site have been designed to provide maximum value and to allow for you to streamline your evaluation. Time, after all, is the most valuable commodity. I want to help you make the best use of it.

Why Should You Listen To Me?

Why should you listen to me, especially when Wall Street and its financial advisors tell you to do the opposite? This is the first question I would be asking if I were you.

I have the good fortune of being a co-founder and partner in the highest rated gold company in the country, *Advantage Gold.* We only work with investors who are acquiring physical gold and other precious metals as part of an overall portfolio, mostly within qualified retirement accounts. Our clients are long term investors, not *traders*. We began the business four years ago with just three employees and since then have become the gold standard of precious metals firms. For the last two years we have won the Trustlink Award, created by the Better Business Bureau, as the highest rated precious metals firm in the country. We have helped our clients acquire hundreds of millions of dollars of precious metals, and have thousands of clients that hail from every state in the country. Today, we employ more than 50 people.

So what makes me believe I have information that can help you? Understanding my backstory may help. Five years ago my life looked very different than it does today. I was not a successful partner of a large national company. In fact, quite the opposite. Five years ago I went through a very difficult time in my life. The entertainment career I had devoted my entire adult life to had hit a dead end. I was in debt, had no real business skills, (I had been in the movie business after all), and had to figure out how I was going to survive. I was at the lowest point in my life, and was searching for answers.

20 years prior, after graduating college, I had narrowed down my future career between two very different paths. I could either get my JD/MBA at one of the top law and business schools in the country, or I could move to Los Angeles and pursue a career in the entertainment business. All of my family and most college friends chose the business or law school route. I took the road less traveled, and moved out west.

My journey in the entertainment business is a story for another book. Suffice to say I believed I was in the midst of a successful career producing movies and developing superhero franchises. I had sold my first big movie to Paramount Studios starring Mark Wahlberg and had forged a partnership with the iconic Stan Lee and the cable giant Comcast to create a new entertainment studio. *On paper,* I was worth millions. I was living my dream, had overcome the odds, and was among the lucky few to find success in the movie business... or so I thought. As quickly as you can say, "Comcast acquires NBC Universal" is how fast things turned upside down for me. Our newly inherited partners at NBC Universal had no interest in our venture. Comcast walked away and I found myself unemployed. I had leveraged my entire future into a partnership that no longer existed. The allure of Hollywood that drew me in 22 years earlier, finally spit me out. I was 43 years old, single, and deeply in debt. I was left to imagine what my life would have become had I gone the more traditional route. I probably would have married and had a successful law or business career like my brothers and most of my college friends. To say that I was going through an existential crisis would be an understatement. My spirit had been broken. I begged God that if he would just show me where to go, I would follow faithfully.

Thankfully, my friend got me a job where he worked selling gold. Little did we know that this moment would change both of our lives forever.

My new job required phoning people and talking to them about the importance of putting physical precious metals inside their IRA's and retirement accounts. On my first day I was handed a one page script, given a phone and told to start dialing. There was only one problem - I had no idea about investments and all I knew about gold was that it was shiny. Selling something I had no experience with scared me. How was I going to recommend something I didn't understand or know anything about? I didn't even know the rules of an IRA or how they worked. Here I was with no training whatsoever, being asked to sell people on something I had no understanding of myself. I would be forced to study on my own if I was going to have any success in this new career I found myself in, which is exactly what I did.

As I began researching, I was immediately struck by one massive surprise: gold had actually outperformed stocks and bonds, and had done so for a very long time. The comparison wasn't even close. Over time, gold had outperformed stocks and bonds 3 to 1. Why was Wall Street so against owning gold? It was this question that I couldn't let go of and it fueled me. My initial cursory study turned into a deep passion to learn everything I could about the ways of Wall Street and investments. Thus began my own personal business school.

I devoted day and night to my new education, consuming everything I could about investments and precious metals. I spent every waking hour researching and studying. I taught myself macroeconomics, interest rates, currencies, and about the flows of capital. I learned about debt, the credit cycle, and how the loosening and tightening of the money supply affected asset values and their prices over time. I then began looking at correlations and what drives markets. I was constantly doing math, trying to find answers. There was no one place to consume this information. I subscribed to dozens of publications, read hundreds of books, and thousands of articles - everything I could get my hands on. Before long, I had become certain that physical gold was an asset that had been completely misrepresented by Wall Street. My new mission was to spread the truth about gold to as many people as I could.

In 2014 I asked my close friend and mentor in the gold business, Kirill, if he would be interested in starting our own company. We wanted to focus on *education* and offer a valuable *service* to our clients. That year we founded Advantage Gold, and have put information at the forefront of everything we do. Every broker in our firm undergoes an intense three month training program. In an effort to further add value for our clients, we even purchased 10,000 copies of the book The New Case For Gold from the acclaimed writer Jim Rickards and *gave them away* to people considering investing in precious metals. Our company has succeeded, in large part, because we lead first by adding value through education. We have learned that the more value we give, the more our business has grown. We are now regarded as the *institutional* standard in a non-regulated, non-institutional environment.

To look at my life and how much it has changed in just five years is astounding. I am fortunate to have excellent partners, each of whom are focused on how we can provide our clients with great education, and offer the highest level of customer experience. Our IRA department is the very best in the entire country, led by Chelsey Jenkins, who ensures that every single transaction is executed with utmost compliance and security. I have the privilege of working with a fantastic team of people who care about what they do and whom I passionately love. I also met and married Charlotte. She is my best friend. Every day I marvel at her beauty, intelligence and humility, and that I am the lucky guy that gets to be in her presence for the rest of our lives.

I have a deep faith that God has made all of this possible. I believe He has placed me in this position so that I can spread this message to you and to as many people as possible. He instilled a passion in me that has only continued to grow deeper, especially as I continue to experience first hand how completely unaware investors are of the important concepts I share in this book. I believe that I was destined to share this information with you. It's information you won't find anywhere else. This is information that Wall Street will never tell you.

The Wall Street Way

If you are like most people, for the last 35 years you've been investing the Wall Street way. The Wall Street way tells us we should put our money in the paper markets and keep it there so our money can go to *work* for us. They say the proper way to invest is to own a selection of stocks and bonds, and, no matter what happens, *stay the course*. Their plan tells us to own these stocks and bonds for *diversification*. They tell us not to own physical gold. They say gold doesn't do anything, it just sits there, doesn't pay dividends, and costs money to store and insure. According to Wall Street, physical gold is for crazy people and conspiracy theorists who think the world is coming to an end.

I believe Wall Street has sold us strategies that are in their best interests, not necessarily in ours. *Stay the course, own stocks and bonds for diversification, and don't buy gold* are among many of the "lessons" investors hear from their financial advisors on a daily basis. Wall Street wants you to believe you are doing the right thing by using their strategies for investing. Even the word *investing* sounds stable and dependable. At young age we are taught that investing is a virtue, and a key component to success in life. We are told we should *invest* in our future.

The definition of investing is: *the devotion of time and energy to an undertaking with the expectation of a favorable result.* This definition of investing has been distorted by Wall Street. There is no reason to believe that financial investing through owning securities (another ironic word) is in any way safe and secure. The truth is that Wall Street uses the word *investing*, but what you are really doing when you own securities is *gambling*.

Gambling implies risk. Risks have never been greater than they are today. Wall Street needs to keep us gambling so they can continue to take the *vigorish*. The vigorish, or "vig" is a term used in casinos and is the percentage deducted from a gambler's winnings by the organizers of the game. In many ways the Wall Street vig is worse than that being taken by casinos offering games of chance. Wall Street gets paid their vig whether we win or lose. Mutual funds carry large expense ratios and financial institutions take assets under management (AUM) fees to *manage* our money, and there are large transaction fees and hidden costs in virtually all paper securities. Wall Street has developed complex financial instruments that they themselves often don't understand, and has sold them to lesser informed people like you and me as the right ways to *secure* our financial futures. There are high frequency computers trading on algorithms tied to complicated leverage strategies that may be incredibly risky. What happens when volatility strikes? Who knows how correlated or risky these underlying *securities* really are? Wall Street doesn't try to explain any of this. We are told their way is good for us. It's better for Wall Street that you don't understand the "securities" they peddle. All the more reason you'll continue to need them and take their advice. They'll do anything to keep you playing the game.

The Math Wall Street Doesn't Want You To Know

If you invested $100,000 in the paper stock and bond markets in January 2000 and received the maximum possible return by reinvesting all of your dividends and then were *lucky* enough to have achieved returns that matched the overall index, today that $100,000 would be worth roughly $320,000. The same $100,000 invested in gold in January 2000 is worth roughly $450,000 in gold today.

Do the calculation yourself. Go to www.goldisabetterway.com

Gold, which is down 33% from highs it reached in 2011, and has been portrayed as only for crazy people and conspiracy theorists, has dramatically outperformed the highest flying stock and bond markets in history.

The title of this book is *Gold Is A Better Way*. The math over the last 17 years confirms the premise. I'll ask an easy question - how much would you rather have: $320,000 or $450,000?

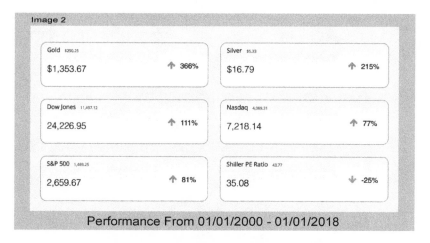

Performance From 01/01/2000 - 01/01/2018

If these lopsided numbers don't wake you up, especially given the current inflated stock and bond bubbles the world finds itself in, then perhaps this book is not for you. If, however, you are like me and find these numbers outrageous, please read on.

There has never been a more important time to consider rebalancing your portfolio. The world economic environment is changing. What has been easy and warm weather for investors over the past decade is about to get cold and more difficult. *It's time for a new strategy.* My aim is to change the narrative and reveal the truth. Gold is not just a bearish asset. Gold is an asset that performs best in an inflationary environment. Gold is an asset that performs best in a debt environment. Gold is an asset necessary to own in an unstable world. Gold is the best asset you can own when other assets have been heavily inflated and manipulated. My goal is that you will walk away after reading this book with one conclusion: **gold is a better way**.

OVERVIEW

"Sometimes all it takes is a tiny shift of perspective to see
something familiar in a totally new light"

Dan Brown

Pain Can Be Good

In 2007 we entered into a recession that was one of the scariest
periods in modern economic history. The Housing Bubble, and
the financial crisis that resulted once it popped, wiped out roughly
$16 Trillion in a mere 18 months. The pain endured during this
time could have served the world well.

Wisdom remembered, taught through thousands of years of
history, could have sparked a massive change in the world's
behavior. The lesson should have been clear: *debt and easy*
credit lead to massive asset bubbles. When these bubbles pop,
the effect can be devastating. That change in behavior could
have been a reduction in debt, a tightening of our belts, and fiscal
responsibility.

Instead of fixing the problem, Central Banks doubled down.
Global sovereign debt in 2008 amounted to $30 Trillion. Today it
stands at over $63 Trillion. We didn't tighten our belts, we did the
opposite and took the belt off altogether. We have been feasting

on cheap money ever since. The result is *The Everything Bubble*.

In 2008, with the world economy on life support, Central Banks jumped in with a defibrillator. They made money free and then printed trillions more of it. They did this by manipulating interest rates to 0% and creating more than $6 Trillion in new money supply.

These actions of Central Banks have created massive distortions. Distortions that have inflated financial assets. Distortions that have allowed the wealthy to get wealthier, are squeezing the middle class, and have left the lower class more worse off. Distortions that have inflated financial assets while creating no real wage inflation. Distortions that have caused populist uprisings around the world from Brexit, to the election of Donald Trump, and the independence of Catalonia. Distortions that will be the genesis of more and more anti-establishment movements in the coming years. Distortions that have forever changed the course of world history. These distortions will have dire consequences.

Every day in America, roughly 175 people die from drug overdoses. What is alarming is that it's estimated that 70% of these deaths are from users who became addicted after being *prescribed* painkillers by their doctors. These people did not die from their original ailments. They died overdosing on the painkillers that were initially meant to *alleviate their pain.* It is the painkillers themselves that ultimately become a deadly problem. In 2008, facing a financial crisis fueled by debt, what did we do? *We prescribed more debt!* This is akin to taking a patient addicted to opiates, tripling their dosage of painkillers, and then expecting it to end well. If the world economy is the patient and the Central Banks are the doctor, the medication they have prescribed is more debt. Financial Oxycontin in the form of borrowed free money. It is a painkiller that has allowed the ailing patient to walk around feeling healthy. It's a false positive and it will ultimately destroy us. Rather than allow the world to suffer through a painful and extended de-leveraging, Central Banks bailed us out.

Pain is necessary to build strength. Pain is a warning that something may not be right. Pain brings clarity and perspective. Pain gives us wisdom. Pain brings us together because it is a shared experience. Pain provides the impetus to learn, to improve, and to grow. Instead of really feeling that pain, we are now addicted to the painkiller of debt.

The good news, in the short term, is that the Central Bank's actions seem to have worked. World equity markets have more than quadrupled since bottoming out in 2009. Housing prices are at all-time highs and the bond market is on a 37-year bull run. These gains in *everything* have lulled almost everyone to sleep, allowing us to believe the patient is healthy. We are not. We are deep inside *The Everything Bubble*.

Has this asset inflation been the result of growth and productivity? Sadly, no. The Everything Bubble has been accomplished through financial engineering. Through stealing from our future to pay for today. The result has been short term gain. The effect will be long term pain.

By addressing the symptoms and not the cause, Central Banks and their actions now are more important to the markets than *value and price discovery*. Stocks and bonds have never been more inflated or more correlated. Investors have never been more challenged. There is no place to hide.

After prescribing a massive dose of free money, and then refilling that prescription continually month after month for nearly 10 years, Central Banks are now faced with a dilemma: take us off the medication or keep it flowing? After 10 years of letting it flow the plan is that Central Banks are turning off the spigots. No longer will they be buying bonds. Now they will actually start selling them as they let bonds roll off their balance sheets. Interest rates will go higher as the phony demand of

Central Banks is withdrawn. There will be blood.

When that happens, what will Central Banks do? Can we expect further rounds of medication? Or will the doctor realize that doing so only further exacerbates the problem and stick with the plan? Regardless of what ultimately occurs, our financial markets are about to undergo a serious sea change.

The definition of inflation, agreed to by most economists is, *too much money chasing too few goods and services*. The Federal Reserve argues that we have very little inflation. It's been their main excuse for keeping interest rates on floor for the last decade. One has to wonder how they can miss the massive inflation in asset prices. If we alter the definition of inflation slightly to, *too much money chasing too few assets*, evidence of inflation is everywhere.

Stocks are up 300% from their bottom and are on a near nine year record-setting bull run. Corporate bonds have never been more attractive to the borrowing corporations and more expensive for the lenders. Subprime corporate junk bonds in Europe pay a meager 2.5% yield. This is for junk!

Central Bankers, with their "fat finger" buying and ultra low interest rates, have eliminated true price discovery across most securities of stocks and bonds. Real estate is at all-time highs in most parts of the United States and in bubble territory in Canada and Australia. The Federal Reserve knows all of this. Their failure to acknowledge it publicly is nothing more than feigned ignorance of the 800 pound gorilla they themselves created.

These loose monetary policies have punished savers and retirees the most. These policies have forced everyday investors to take on more risk in search of yield and higher returns. These policies have led to *too much money chasing too few assets*. It has all led to an inflationary bubble that The Federal Reserve has created, and one Wall Street has been complicit in taking advantage of; trillions of dollars of easy money, all going to financial assets.

While financial assets have massively inflated, the prices of *real goods and commodities* have deflated. Commodities have fallen over 35%. Silver is down roughly 70% from highs of around $49 per ounce and has been hovering in the $16-to $17 range per ounce. Gold is down from highs of over $1,900 per ounce and has remained range bound between $1,200 - $1,350 per ounce in the past few years.

This is all about to reverse. We have begun to see signs of a synchronized global recovery. GDP is picking up. The inflation that has been so desperately missing in the last decade appears to be on its way back. This growth trend, while heading in a positive direction, is far from a deep recovery. The global recovery will likely continue to remain sluggish. It will be handcuffed by the massive overhang of debt.

What's ironic is that Wall Street wants to suggest that this recent uptrend in growth will be good for your portfolio. It won't. They want you focused on the growth story when portfolios have already risen to thin air and want to argue that they will continue higher from here. What Wall Street won't tell you is that real growth at this point may actually be a negative if you are an investor in the financial markets. The market quadrupled over ten years with zero growth. *Real growth* is the *worst thing* that can happen to your portfolio right now. It means the free money and financial engineering from Central Banks will be pulled away. Real growth will force Central Banks hands to continue tightening monetary policy and letting air out of the balloon.

If it was the "loose" policies that allowed it all to occur in the first place, it's the "tightening" of those policies that will cause the Everything Bubble to pop. They say a picture is worth a thousand words. I will let three images tell this story:

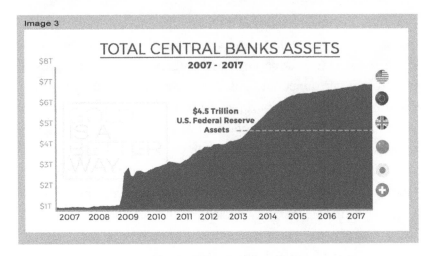

Prior to 2008 the Federal Reserve held roughly $800 Billion in assets on their balance sheet. Today the assets on the Federal Reserve's balance sheet have ballooned to over $4.5 Trillion. Why the sudden and massive growth? This is how money gets printed in today's world. The Federal Reserve and other Central Banks "print" new money through a *bond buying* program called Quantitative Easing.

Here's how it works: The Fed "buys bonds" from the Treasury and then deposits the money for the "purchase" of those bonds into the Treasury's coffers. It's a magic trick that's akin to taking money from your left pocket and putting it into your right pocket, and then counting it as new money. This *newly created money* is then available for the Treasury to lend. The Federal Reserve counts these bonds as "assets" on their balance sheet. This magic trick allows Central Banks to print trillions of dollars in new money while also manipulating interest rates lower. Image 3 indicates how much new money has been created since 2008. Image 4 shows how virtually all of this money has gone to the stock market.

From 2008 through 2016 The Fed and other Central Banks have consistently printed new money and continued their low interest rate policies. Image 4 shows that virtually all of the new

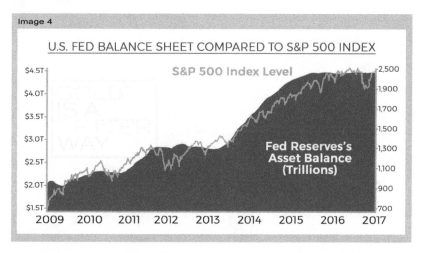

U.S. FED BALANCE SHEET COMPARED TO S&P 500 INDEX

money that was printed went directly to one place: the stock market. Is the stock market up 300% because of tremendous economic growth? Clearly not. The market is higher for one main reason: newly printed Central Bank created money has flowed into the equity markets.

This is why I am so confident that now is a great time to sell the market. A seasonal change is now upon us. The Federal Reserve is now unwinding its balance sheet. Instead of *Quantitative Easing*, they are now *Quantitative Tightening*. Their plan is to tighten the money supply and allow interest rates to rise. Image 5 shows us that the plan is for Central Banks to begin dumping assets onto the market. In the exact way that Quantitative Easing allowed the stock market to soar higher, Quantitative Tightening will most likely cause the stock market to dive lower.

The story for those paying attention is clear: the bubbles created through Central Bank debt explosion have allowed financial assets to hit all-time highs and have created the Everything Bubble. It is the *tightening* of credit and *rising interest rates* that will cause these bubbles to pop. The result will be defaults.

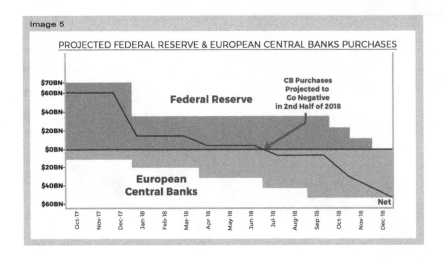

Image 5

PROJECTED FEDERAL RESERVE & EUROPEAN CENTRAL BANKS PURCHASES

These defaults will be similar to what occurred in 2008 as credit tightened and markets collapsed in the wake of the financial crisis. Those adhering to the Wall Street way, who *stayed invested* when the housing bubble popped in 2008, experienced massive declines in their portfolio value as stocks plummeted. Staying fully invested is a fine strategy when everything goes up. It can be a devastating strategy when everything comes down.

As credit tightens over the coming years it will put massive downward pressures on stock and bonds. These pressures will lead to valuation loss and defaults. The loser when these defaults occur will be dollar-inflated paper assets. The winner when this occurs will be tangible real assets like gold. It is the foolish man who builds his house on sand. In this case the sand of debt, deficits, and inflated paper assets. It is the wise man who builds his house on the rock solid foundation of the oldest money known to man: **gold**.

GOLDEN NUGGET #1
Things that make you go "Hmmm..."

Which Comes First, Dow 50,000 or Gold $2,600 per ounce?

Historically we endure a recession every seven years or so. A recession is defined as a 20% or more drop in stock prices. The last recession in 2008 saw the stock market drop 57%. The recession in 2000 saw a drop in equity markets of 47%. The average recession, historically, has equaled 35%.

We are currently on a nine-year bull run without a recession. In 2017 the Dow Jones hit record new highs 73 times. Today the index is just shy of 25,000 points, posting an annual gain of 5,000 points in 2017. So, from this point forward, which doubles first, gold or the Dow? It's an interesting question to ponder.

Let's assume the Dow hits 30,000 points by the year 2020. Factoring in recessions of 25%, (dramatically lower than the average of 35%), every seven years the Dow would not hit 50,000 points until the year 2033.

Conversely, gold was $284 per ounce in the year 2000 and at the end of 2017 stood at a price of $1,296 per ounce. This is an increase of 358% and an annual increase of 11.1%. If we factored in average growth in the price of gold at 11% per year, gold would hit $2,600 per ounce in the year 2023. Based strictly on past 18 year averages, gold will be at $2,600 per ounce roughly 10 years before the Dow hits 50,000 points.*

*Past performance is not indicative of future results

19

I HISTORY - BEFORE FIAT

1 THE MONEY OF KINGS

"He who has the gold makes the rules"

Donald Trump when asked why his home decor includes
so much gold

What Is Money?

One of my first clear memories of learning in school was when I was 12 years old and in the 7th Grade. My teacher, Sister Kathleen, on the first semester of school, gave a lesson about the value of money. It's one I have forever remembered.

Sister Kathleen separated the class into five different groups and announced, "Our group project is that we are going to make ham and cheese sandwiches. The team that makes the best sandwich wins." She then pulled out various ingredients. A loaf of bread, a block of cheese, a pound of sliced ham, a jar of mayonnaise and several tomatoes were provided, with each group receiving a different ingredient. She then informed us of the rules. "Each team's sandwich must have every ingredient in order to qualify. May the best sandwich win," she proclaimed.

At first none of us knew what to do. My team was given the block of cheese. How were we going to make a ham and cheese sandwich from a block of cheese? It wasn't long before we realized each group had a necessary ingredient for the sandwich we were required to make. Within seconds it was mayhem as two dozen 12 year olds began running back and forth yelling and bartering for what each team needed.

This was my first school lesson on economics and the progression of the early barter system. Sister Kathleen used the lesson as a way to highlight that early farmer civilizations had to trade with one another for various commodities. She explained that some farmers raised cows whose milk was necessary to make cheese. Other farmers raised pigs. Other farmers had crops and the necessary grains to make bread and vegetable farmers grew produce. In order for each farmer to get other necessary supplies, they would need to trade with one another. As a class we quickly understood the challenges associated with the barter system. We were then asked what would make the barter system we had just experienced easier. The answer was clear to our 12 year old minds: money.

The next day Sister Kathleen repeated the exercise with the class. Only this time she brought in a large stack of Monopoly money and handed each group the same amount. Once again she repeated the rules that we all must make sandwiches with every ingredient, only this time added, "the team with the most money in the end wins."

Now we discovered a different problem. After several trades it became apparent that some ingredients were more valuable than others. Ham and cheese were most valuable, followed by the bread, with mayonnaise and tomatoes bringing up the rear and ascribed the least value. We comically went back and forth trading our money between ourselves, all trying to gather the most important and necessary ingredients for the winning sandwich. My group had the cheese, and it was easy to get more money for our cheese since it was the number one ingredient every team wanted. As a result, my team in the end not only had the most money, we also had the best sandwich since we were able to buy all the necessary ingredients from every other team.

Team Tomato cried that the game was unfair because nobody was willing to pay as much for tomatoes as they were for cheese and ham. Day Two's lesson illuminated the value of each commodity, and how the more valuable commodities provided certain teams more power as they were able to command a higher price for their goods.

On the third day we repeated the exercise. This time with another twist. At this point in the game my team had the vast majority of the money, with Team Ham in second place. Team Tomato had no money whatsoever. On day three, Sister Kathleen pulled out a new and even bigger stack of Monopoly money, and to every other teams chagrin, gave it all to Team Tomato. Sister Kathleen informed us that Team Tomato was now also the Central Bank, and could add as much money as they wanted to the Ham and Cheese Economy. She then pulled out wads of Monopoly money and gave it all to Team Tomato to use however they wanted.

Team Ham and my team eventually cried, "No way, not fair," as Team Tomato added money to the system. The day before we were the most powerful two teams. We had most of the money and our money had great value. Now, as money was handed out freely by the Central Bank of Tomato, our money became less and less valuable. It was a great lesson on inflation and the devaluation of money.

On day four Sister Kathleen changed the game again, this time by adding 100 copper pennies to the system. Back then a cent was actually worth something and we were all excited that "real" money had been added to the game. Now, as money was handed out freely by the Central Bank of Tomato, our entire Ham and Cheese economy became unstable. Prices fluctuated and nobody was certain of the actual value of the money in the system.

From here a fascinating thing happened: within minutes a count of all the paper money in the game was conducted. The Central Bank of Team Tomato was still able to add as much paper money as they wanted to the system. Only now, when measured against the static value of the 100 pennies, adding more paper money only made it more worthless. Providing a fixed constant allowed for stability and certainty in the new economy.

On the fifth day Sister Kathleen turned the game upside down one last time. She depleted the amount of pennies in the system by 50%. Just as we had learned how adding paper money to the system on Day Three and Four created instability and inflation, now on Day Five we learned about deflation. With less currency in the system our money was now more powerful and prices went down as a result.

This lesson, while quite simple in execution, was one of the most compelling lessons I have ever learned about economies and why the supply of money is so important to their overall function.

The Value Of Money

How could I have predicted that one day I would be recounting this childhood experience as an introduction to my book and the subject of gold? I sometimes wonder had I not gone through that exercise as a young boy would I be writing a book about gold at all, or would I be as passionate about the subject today?

The main impact of my childhood school lesson was that money is more valuable when there is a limited supply. As paper money was added to our Ham and Cheese System, that money became less and less valuable. By subtracting money from the supply, prices went down and our money had more value. Only after adding a static and consistent standard of the physical pennies into the mix, was the financial system stable and able to be controlled. I believe this story is a good introduction to gold.

Gold is static and unchanging. It is this exact feature that makes gold more relevant today than at any time in history. It is what allowed gold to become money 5,000 years ago as early barter systems became untenable. It's what we will go back to in the future when the monetary system fails.

Gold Remains The Basis Of The Monetary System

The top ten Central Banks around the world today own a combined 23,000 tons of gold. The IMF owns 2,000 tons making for a round total of 25,000 tons of gold. This gold represents about 12% of all the gold ever mined. A testament to gold's durability is that virtually every ounce of gold ever mined is still above ground. Gold is among the rarest of all of the elements making up only three parts per billion of the earth's crust. There are 325 million people in the United States. Trying to find gold is like trying to find one person in the entire U.S. population.

Gold weighs 19 times more than water and is twice as heavy as lead. Over 90% of physical gold in existence has been mined since the California gold rush. The total gold mined in history is estimated to be about 188,000 tons. This means that all of the gold mined in the history of mankind would fit into two Olympic sized swimming pools.

One of the biggest arguments against gold is that it doesn't provide any return. That's correct, and is exactly one of the most compelling reasons to own it in my opinion. Gold does not pay any return because gold has no risk. A $100 bill doesn't pay any return either unless you deposit it into a bank, at which point it has risk because it is now a *liability* of the bank. You are the creditor and the $100 deposited into the bank now has a risk that the bank may or may not return your $100. While the gold price can go up and can go down, the elemental and static nature of gold is its greatest feature because it is constant and therefore has no risk of permanent impairment. Permanent loss of value is a risk that all financial assets have. Gold will always be gold and has no such risk. It's for these reasons that gold first became money.

Money ultimately must have three components:

1. Unit of Account: measures the cost of an economic item
2. Medium of Exchange: an intermediary instrument used to facilitate the purchase or trade of goods between parties
3. Store of Value: an asset that can be saved, exchanged, and retrieved at a later time

Today there are several different forms of money, including the Dollar, the Euro, the Yuan, and other national currencies. Digital currencies like Bitcoin and Ethereum can also be considered money. Gold it turns out is the *perfect* form of money.

Gold As Currency

The purpose of this book is not to be a history of gold and paper money, but more an evaluation of how gold performs, especially when considered against paper currencies and other financial assets. Understanding gold's backstory however, is relevant to understanding gold's future. The properties of gold that made it the perfect form for money are the same today as they were 5,000 years ago. They are as follows:

1. Gold is Scarce
2. Gold is Exchangeable
3. Gold is Divisible
4. Gold is Incorruptible
5. Gold is Portable

It is these physical properties of gold that were the very reason gold became the foundation of the global monetary system. Before travel and commerce between nations was commonplace, each nation individually settled on gold as the perfect form of money. As nations grew independently and then began trading, the scarce, static, consistent, and pure nature of gold made it the perfect form of money acceptable for trading. Its consistency was its greatest feature and evened out all accounting and price systems.

Gold Is Practical

Anyone familiar with the periodic table of elements from high school will remember that there are a finite number of known elements in the universe. Each known element has an atomic symbol and atomic number that measures the number of protons in their nucleus. The atomic symbol for gold is Au and it has an atomic number of 78. Gold gets its name from the Latin word *aurum* meaning gold. Gold (Au) is a physical element, plain and simple. Its properties are static and will never change. Gold has been a physical element for billions of years and will continue to be billions of years in the future.

In his excellent book *The New Case For Gold*, Jim Rickards highlights the research of Andrea Sella, a professor of chemistry at the University of London. Sella discusses the practicality of using gold as money in the physical world.

Professor Sella shows us that most of the matter in the universe would be ineffective as a use for money. He walks through the periodic table and eliminates helium, argon and other gases as having no weight, and therefore useless as money. He also goes through and rejects mercury and bromine as they are liquid at room temperature and are as impractical as gases. Sella eliminates toxic and poisonous elements like arsenic. The twelve alkaline elements ranging from magnesium to sodium are also impractical as they dissolve or explode on contact with water. He then eliminates radioactive elements like plutonium and thorium. Sella further takes other elements like copper and iron out of contention as they corrode when exposed to air over time.

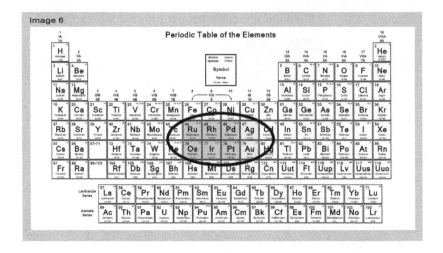

Once all the aforementioned elements have been eliminated we are left with the metals situated in the middle of the table which could even be considered for money based on their elemental properties. These elements include iridium, osmium, ruthenium, platinum, palladium, rhodium, silver and gold.

According to Sella, "That leaves us with two elements to consider for use of money, silver and gold. Both are scarce but not impossibly rare. Both have relatively low melting points and are therefore easy to turn into coins, ingots, and jewelry. Silver tarnishes when it reacts with minute amounts of sulphur in the air. That's why we place particular value on gold."

Rickards then adds the obvious, "Gold also happens to be beautiful."

Gold Is Biblical

Biblical records show that gold and silver are the oldest form of money and have never failed in over 5,000 years. The book of Genesis spans 2,400 years and tells the story of the creation of man, God's instructions on how to live and where to find the essentials for living. Genesis 2:12 says, "The gold of the land is good." If you believe in the Bible and its teachings, God wanted man to have gold for a reason. The reason we can gather was so that man could use it as money. Gold is mentioned in the Bible 417 times. Silver is mentioned in the Bible 320 times. Money is mentioned in the Bible 140 times, each time referring to either silver or gold.

Gold and silver are referred throughout the Bible as representing real wealth from its first book of Genesis through its last book of Revelations. The Bible tells us that gold and silver are the only God-ordained monetary assets that will maintain their purchasing power until the day of the Lord's wrath.

When Moses ascended the mountain at Sinai to commune with God, he was given the ten commandments which are carried in the *golden* arc. When the Israelites broke the law by worshiping a *golden* calf, God sent a plague as punishment. Moses was surrounded by a strong *golden light* that no one could look upon him.

Gold in the Bible is likened to wisdom, faith and knowledge. In the book of Psalms it says that God's laws and commandments are more valuable than gold. Gold is considered by the Bible to be the most valuable thing one can possess behind knowledge, faith, and righteousness. Perhaps the most well known reference to gold in the Bible is from the story of the Magi and the gifts they presented to the baby Jesus. The wise men offered gifts of gold, frankincense and myrrh. Gold representing Kingship on earth.

The name Christ is derived from the Greek meaning *golden one*. Revelations 21:21 tells us, "The greatest street of the city was pure gold." Jesus' greatest command was, "Do unto others as you would have them do unto you," and is referred to as the *Golden Rule*.

The earliest biblical mention to what gold could *purchase* is from Daniel 2, and references the reign of King Nebuchadnezzar from 600 BC. We learn from Daniel that a one ounce gold coin during this time would buy 350 loaves of bread. The current price of a loaf of bread today is about $3.50. Notice that an ounce of gold from the year 600 BC purchases roughly the same amount of bread 2600 years later. Gold was never intended to make one rich, but rather *preserve* one's buying power.

Throughout the course of history, the amount of new gold mined has averaged 1.5% annually. The historical growth of the human population has also averaged 1.5% annually. Atheists may consider this a coincidence. For those of faith it's as if God created the perfect form of money for mankind to use and also accounted for mankind's future growth ensuring there would always be enough new money supply to meet the growth in population.

Gold Is Desired

The Latin word for gold is *aurum* which means *shining dawn*. In the beautiful words of Mark Cartwright, "That which the sun radiates around itself as light and warmth as a force for the soul and the earth." The mighty sun aura which rays out over the whole cosmos is concentrated in gold. It's what the early Romans called *aurum,* since gold is very condensed sunlight. Aurum being a concentrated aura.

In Greek society, gold represented power and wealth. In Greek mythology King Midas was rewarded with a wish that all he touched would turn into gold. This nearly leads to Midas' own death and starvation as even his food turns to gold. In his quest for wealth and power he had forgotten the importance of the simple necessities in life.

The Ancient Egyptians mined huge quantities of gold. Africa has immense gold reserves and is the site of the fabled mines of King Solomon and his lost city of gold. The early Egyptians used gold to decorate their temples. The tombs of their pharaohs who were believed to be the reincarnation of their sun god were laden with gold.

The Aztecs regarded gold as a symbol of their sun god and crafted intricate gifts of gold to give as offerings. Their entire culture would ultimately fall because of gold and the Spanish Conquistadors' greed. Cortes, after finding tons of gold, took the Aztec King Montezuma hostage, promising to only release him for a room of gold. The natives were surprised as gold was so plentiful and complied with the request, providing the Spaniards with several tons of gold. That gold was transported to Spain, melted down, and still today decorates many of the catholic churches in Spain. Cortes then betrayed the Aztecs and had Montezuma murdered. The Aztec civilization never recovered from this betrayal.

Gold In The Psyche Of Mankind

Gold is associated with winners. When an Olympic athlete comes in first place they are awarded a *gold medal*. Gold is associated with achievement and success. The height of wisdom in civilizations is referred to as the *Golden Age*. It turns out that still today gold is one of the most valuable and sought after commodities in the world.

Gold: The Foundation Of America

Prior to the California Gold Rush in 1849, The United States of America was really a collection of farmer states along the eastern seaboard. A newly colonized people that were in the process of attempting to become united, with each individual state's egoism trumping the national organization. Gold would play a primary role in establishing the United States as a world superpower.

The discovery of gold at Sutter's Mill in California on January

24th, 1848 would change the future face of America forever. The California Gold Rush was the impetus for the largest mass migration in American history. More than 300,000 people would head west in search of a better way of life made possible by gold.

The discovery of gold in the west would allow for the development of the western United States and have a massive impact on California. The gold rush propelled California from a sleepy backwater to the center of global imagination and the destination of hundreds of thousands of people around the globe.

The gold rush's new wealth and population migration led to the improved transportation systems between the east and the west coasts. The Panama Railway (precursor to the Panama Canal) would be built linking the Atlantic Ocean to the Pacific Ocean and be finished in 1855. Steamships would begin regular service from San Francisco to Panama where passengers, mail, and goods would make their way across, thereafter boarding steamships headed to the East Coast. The desire for gold was so great that new state of the art transportation routes and systems were built in order to facilitate access to the precious metal.

The gold rush would bring gold seekers from every country and corner of the world. It would stimulate California's economy and establish America as the *land of opportunity.* A place where with good fortune and the discovery of gold, one could go from poverty to wealth overnight.

Gold also provided the impetus for something much more powerful. As a nation, America had *new money* that provided for a newfound wealth and prosperity. The discovery of gold in California would be the birth of a powerful America that would ultimately set the foundation for the current monetary system.

2   POWER

"When money speaks, the truth keeps silent"

Carl Sandberg

World War I

The balance of gold reserves that made America a main player on the world stage after the gold rush would soon grow disproportionately to the rest of the world with the advent of the First World War. The war was initially known as the European War and only after World War II would it be called World War I.

The war pitted the Central Powers of Germany, Austria-Hungary and Turkey against the Allies, who were France, Great Britain, Russia, Italy and Japan. The United States, which had been growing in power, stayed out of the war during the first two and half years, openly debating whether it was our war to fight. President Woodrow Wilson declared that the U.S. would remain neutral.

For the first years of the fight remaining neutral helped the United States become a world superpower as she was in position to sell American goods to both sides of the battle. Staying neutral allowed for the American economy to boom. We sold materials, munitions, commodities and other goods to both sides of the European fight. As supplies headed out, gold flowed in.

The gold pouring in allowed the United States to build massive reserves. As gold flowed into America, it flowed out of Europe. The embattled superpowers of Europe would watch their gold coffers become depleted as the war raged on. The First World War did more than shift the balance of power in Europe, it also shifted the balance of gold holdings, allowing the United States to build the largest gold reserves of any other country in the world. By the time America entered World War I, the European Superpowers had already been monumentally damaged economically, demographically, and they held far less gold.

The war resulted in a changed geopolitical landscape and the destruction of three Empires. New borders were drawn in Europe at the end of the war. The ongoing frustration with the European restructuring decisions made after fighting ceased would eventually lead to World War II.

The after effects of World War I meant that America was now a power unlike any other. The United States emerged as a super-state, exercising a veto power over the financial and security concerns of other major countries in the world. Adam Tooze, in his book *The Deluge*, explains how gold played an integral role in allowing the United States to become the world's greatest power. Tooze suggests that it was failure of the United States to cooperate with the efforts of French, British, Japanese and Germans to stabilize a viable world economy and to establish new institutions of collective security in the 1920's and 1930's that allowed for the ongoing instability that would be a major cause of the Great Depression and thereafter World War II. The reason was simple: the rest of the world needed the U.S. because we had the vast majority of the gold. It turns out America was too focused on her own agenda to care.

Every other World War I belligerent had quit the gold standard at the beginning of the war. As part of their war finance effort, they accepted that their currencies would depreciate against gold.

Naturally the currencies of the losers depreciated more than the currencies of the winners. At the end of the conflict every national government had to decide whether to return to the gold standard and, if so, at what rate.

Everyone except Great Britain chose to leave the gold standard. For the 330 years prior to World War I, the British Empire was the greatest superpower the world had ever known, covering a quarter of the world's surface. So powerful was the British Empire that the sun never set on it. It turned out that gold would play a large part in the undoing of The British Empire. They would re-peg their British Pound back to pre-war gold prices rather than pegging it to a higher gold price, thereby overvaluing their currency and setting off widespread global deflation.

After World War I, the United States catapulted to the position of the world's leading creditor, the world's largest owner of gold, and by extension the effective custodian of the gold standard. One important result in the balance of gold reserves would go on to rebound on America in a negative way. America's ongoing determination to maintain the U.S. Dollar *as good as gold* not only imposed terrible hardship on war ravaged Europe, it also flooded the American markets with low-cost European imports.

The imbalance of gold, and thereby money, is what ultimately led to The Great Depression. Prices lowered as less and less people had access to money. Remember, inflation is too much money chasing too few goods. The Great Depression was fueled by the opposite, deflation, which can be defined as too little money chasing too many goods and services.

Federal Reserve - Paper Notes

The Federal Reserve was created in 1913 when President Woodrow Wilson signed the Federal Reserve Act into law. It was founded by Congress with the intention of providing a more flexible and stable monetary system. The idea of The Fed was to help promote a strong U.S. economy. Prior to The Federal Reserve's creation, the American nation was plagued with a series of panics and bank runs. A severe panic in 1907 resulted in investors rushing to withdraw deposits from local banks which then caused a financial crisis and deep recession.

Congress directed The Fed to conduct the nation's monetary policy to support three main goals: maximum stable employment, stable prices, and to moderate long term interest rates.

In 1913 The Federal Reserve created new bank notes called Federal Reserve Notes. The issuance of these paper notes would set off an economic boom in the United States. More money was printed and circulated. Once free of the restrictions created by physical coinage and its limited supply, the quantity of dollars in circulation multiplied and led to a boom of the roaring twenties in the United States. Like any artificially induced stimulus, it eventually came to a crash in 1929. The culprit? The burden of over-extended credit.

Prior to The Fed's creation, money in circulation consisted of gold, silver and copper coinage, silver notes and gold certificates. These former gold notes issued by the United States bore no-interest and had no debt associated with their issuance. Debt creation prior to 1913 was much more limited and bank lending standards required true and tangible collateral in the form of real money or property.

The newly created Federal Reserve notes were lent out by banks *with interest due*. In the 1920's American citizens took on more debt, helping to create the foundation for the boom of the 1920's. With the amount of Reserve Notes growing and banks more willing to lend, an American expansion fueled by debt occurred. As these notes became more accepted, few members of the general public would ever exchange these paper notes for gold. This permitted The Federal Reserve to lend even more freely without regard to losses or real collateral.

When the interest burden of all of this newly created money began to weigh heavily on the general economy, it led to a credit contraction, that in turn led to the Great Depression and stock market crash of 1929. Suddenly people were reluctant to borrow, banks were reluctant to lend, and velocity of money in circulation slowed.

Confiscation Act Of 1933

Under the gold standard, the gold price had been fixed at $20.67. Citizens began to lose faith in paper dollars in the early 1930's since the actual market value for physical gold began creeping above this fixed price, an indication that confidence in paper notes was starting to wane. A run on the banks and gold was inevitable.

Holders of paper money began redeeming their paper certificates and withdrawing actual physical gold from their banks. The newly created gold fractional reserve system, allowed for by the printing of Federal Reserve Notes, was on the brink of collapse. The Federal Reserve had printed far too many notes than were backed by physical gold. Anyone who's seen the movie *It's A Wonderful Life* may remember the iconic scene where George Bailey uses his personal honeymoon funds to appease the shareholders of the credit union who have *run on the bank* demanding money that wasn't there.

Bank runs became more frequent as individuals lost further faith in the banking system and began redeeming their Federal Reserve Notes for physical gold. Records indicate that the total gold on reserve in 1933 had a market value of $4 Billion and was equal to roughly 6,000 tons. The combined total of gold certificates and Federal Reserve notes amounted to more than 20,000 tons of gold, providing a naked shortfall of nearly 15,000 metric tons of gold.

By way of Executive Order on March 9th, 1933 Franklin Delano Roosevelt made private ownership of gold illegal. U.S. gold certificates would no longer be considered legal tender. Gold and gold certificates were required by law to be turned in and exchanged for Federal Reserve Notes. The U.S. Treasury then sent gold and certificates to the Federal Reserve in exchange for Reserve Notes.

In a famous fireside chat via radio Roosevelt explained his Executive Order to the people. He framed it: "The decision every upstanding American citizen needed to comply with for the good of the nation." Virtually all of the gold in the hands of Americans was then exchanged for paper Federal Reserve Notes.

Then, in one stroke of a pen, once all the gold had been collected, Roosevelt raised the official price of gold from $20.67 to $35 per ounce. This would amount to 80% inflation overnight. Agreement from economists and historians is universal that this one act allowed to shift the ongoing global deflationary environment. Prices would soon rise thereafter. The dollar devalued and gold jumped 80% in the blink of an eye. This act of devaluation is an important lesson to remember in today's world, should a new deflationary environment ever return in the future. If deflation rears its ugly head again, count on gold prices to surge higher as currencies must ultimately deflate in order to combat.

After amassing roughly 10,000 tons of gold from its citizens, the United States would be the holder of the largest gold hoard in the world, with an estimated 15,000 tons of gold in reserves.

The New Golden Rule - "He Who Has The Gold Makes The Rules"

In July 1944 the leaders of the now United Allied Nations of the world gathered in Bretton Woods, New Hampshire. They would leave this convention with a new system for monetary and exchange rate management. Delegates from 44 countries met with the main goal ensuring a foreign exchange rate system and to prevent competitive devaluations.

A new system of fixed exchange rates against the U.S. Dollar was established and the dollar became the international reserve currency of the world. Every major currency would now peg itself to the U.S. Dollar. In turn, and in order to ensure to the rest of the world that its currency was dependable, the U.S. would peg the dollar to gold at the price of $35 per ounce.

In order to ensure compliance with the new rules, two new international institutions were created; The International Monetary Fund (IMF) and The World Bank. Under the Bretton Woods Agreement, foreign governments would continue to be permitted to exchange U.S. Currency reserves for gold at any time, even though it was illegal for individual American citizens to own.

The main challenge in this new system for every other country of the world would be if the United States were ever to devalue the dollar. In 1958 this is exactly what occurred. U.S. expansionary monetary policies increased the supply of dollars. The United States had been through the Korean War and were entering the war in Vietnam in earnest and needed to expand the monetary base to cover the costs associated with these wars.

True to concerns of every other nation, the dollar began to devalue. Foreign governments holding reserves of U.S. Dollars began redeeming them in exchange for physical gold stored in the United States. From 1958 to 1971, 7,000 tons of gold were shipped out of the United States to foreign governments, dramatically depleting United States gold reserves. The war in Vietnam was ramping up and America was facing a serious recession. This caused gold redemptions from foreign governments to surge and forced President Nixon to take drastic action.

On August 15th, 1971 President Richard Nixon would take

the United States off the gold standard. The gold window was now officially closed and foreign governments would no longer be able to redeem dollar reserves for gold. After 27 years the Bretton Woods agreement was officially dead. At the time of the Executive Order, the United States had only 8,000 tons of gold remaining in her coffers.

Since 1971, the dollar has experienced a large devaluation and suffered from serious bouts of inflation. The gold price which was $40 per ounce in 1971, would surge to $800 per ounce by 1979. Over the past 48 years, the price of gold has fluctuated from a low of $35 per ounce to a high of $1,924 per ounce. As of January 1st, 2018 the price of gold is $1,296 per ounce.

Prior to 1971 the value of gold in dollars was static. From the 1800's to 1933 the price of gold stood at $20 per ounce. From 1933 to 1971 the price of gold was $35 per ounce. Since we abandoned the gold standard in 1971 we have witnessed an explosive growth in the world's paper money supply. All of this additional supply of money has been the catalyst for dramatic inflation.

Full Faith And Credit

This is the whole reason to be looking at gold today. While we are no longer on a gold standard, gold is still the standard by which our currency is measured since gold is priced in dollars. Our dollar is no longer backed by reserves of gold. Instead our dollars are now backed by the *full faith and credit of the United States.* That *full faith and credit* of the United States is about to be pressured like never before. As a result our dollars will need to continue to devalue as we head deeper and deeper into debt.

GOLDEN NUGGET #2

Things that make you go "Hmmm..."

Gold $10,000 per ounce? Sound crazy? Think again!

There are long term trends that have continued to play out over history. One of the most eerily consistent is the *inverse relationship between commodities and equities.*

Massive cycles continue to play out and allow for long term investors to see trends and price levels that represent attractive buying opportunities. Commodities look incredibly cheap compared to stocks. The fundamental case for investing in commodities is also well supported. Global economic activity is increasing. Tax cuts, fiscal stimulus and infrastructure spending are inflationary pressures that should allow commodities to significantly outperform equities from this point forward over the coming years. Historically, when commodities are this cheap they outperform equities by an 8:1 ratio in the coming years.

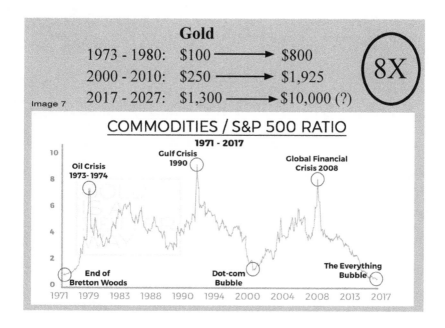

Gold

1973 - 1980:	$100 ⟶	$800
2000 - 2010:	$250 ⟶	$1,925
2017 - 2027:	$1,300 ⟶	$10,000 (?)

8X

Image 7

COMMODITIES / S&P 500 RATIO

1971 - 2017

Oil Crisis 1973-1974 · End of Bretton Woods · Gulf Crisis 1990 · Dot-com Bubble · Global Financial Crisis 2008 · The Everything Bubble

II

WHERE WE ARE

3   ARE YOU HEALTHY?

"I am in shape! Round is a shape!"

John Candy

What The Wise Man Does At The Beginning, The Fool Does In The End

I recently went through an in-depth medical examination where I saw seven different doctors in two days. I am 48 years old and newly married and wanted to get deep and comprehensive overview of my health.

I was given extensive laboratory testing that included blood counts and chemistry panels to assess my organ function with urinalysis and cholesterol screening. I was given a cardiovascular assessment that included an electrocardiograms, electron beam coronary CT scan/angiogram, cardiopulmonary exercise testing and advanced blood tests with carotid intima medial thickness scanning. I was given Doppler flow peripheral vascular index testing. I was also given hearing and eye tests, body composition testing and a personalized nutrition counseling session.

It took two full days of time to do all of the tests that were performed. Thankfully I can report that I passed with flying colors. While I have always taken fairly good care of myself I had shunned doctors visits for a long time. Undergoing these tests was stressful and not at all fun.

In hindsight it turned out to be a great experience. Knowing that my tests came back normal and that my levels were within a healthy range has allowed me the peace of mind to feel like I am in fine shape and have no serious issues to be concerned about, or at least that are detectable. Putting off doctor visits for so long prior left me with a subconscious stress. Receiving a clean bill of health erased all of that worry.

There are a lot of tests one can do to measure physical health. What tests can we do to measure the levels of our investments and the strength or weakness of our financial health? What are considered normal or healthy levels for the assets we invest in?

Are you stressed about your financial future? Are your investments healthy? Wouldn't it be great to have something more to hold on to than just hope? Hope, after all, is not a strategy.

I have spoken to thousands of people about this very question, from retirees to doctors, lawyers and engineers, to government employees, teachers, union workers and hundreds of other professionals. Fortunately for me, my business allows me to meet people from all walks of life with various backgrounds, skills and income levels. Of the thousands of people I have spoken to, very few have a *specific process* to make this evaluation.

The best most of us can do is to say 'I feel good' or 'I don't feel good.' A *feeling* is not a great measurement tool for health or finance. If we wait until we feel bad, often times it's too late. The goal is to act in advance of feeling and with a *system or strategy* that allows for success regardless of *feelings*.

Many investors I speak with tell me that they are *feeling* good or bad about their investments because of how they have performed in the past. They'll say that the market is up or down and either 'I'm making money' or 'I'm not.' These investors are judging past performance and the good or bad feeling with seeing their account balances grow or decline. Investment decisions, just like health decisions, need to be forward looking.

One of my best friend's father took exceptional care of himself. Every morning he would take his supplements and vitamins, go for a brisk 5 mile walk, sit down in his home office afterward and eat a healthy breakfast. Then he would read his Bible. One morning, after following his tried and tested routine he went into cardiac arrest. With no warning he passed away. He was 62 years old. He had left the house that morning *feeling* great. While he *felt* he was in excellent shape had no idea that his arteries were 90% clogged and that he could have gone into cardiac arrest at any time. He couldn't *feel* his health risks.

Investments are similar in that they may feel good as they move higher in value. In today's market you may feel invincible about your investments. This perhaps has never been more true for investors than today. During this run up in the Everything Bubble virtually every financial asset has increased in value.

Do you have a balanced diet in your investments? Do you have expectations based on past performance or are you looking ahead and anticipating what is coming next?

It's never been more challenging than today to obtain unbiased information. In today's social media and fake news world much of the information we receive is skewed to our particular tastes based on algorithms designed so that advertisers can find us more easily.

Confirmation bias is a scientifically proven phenomena. It means that when we make decisions we tend to look for information and evidence that is supportive of what *we have already decided to do*. Said another way, we tend to predict what we root for. Confirmation bias with our investments can be very dangerous as it allows for less objectivity about the reality surrounding us.

A recent, non-scientific 'Internet search' study was performed with three individuals, a Conservative, a Liberal and a Moderate. The Conservative loved red meat and was often online looking at nearby steakhouses and recipes for cooking red meat. The Liberal was health conscious and often searched online for healthy lifestyle choices, and the Moderate loved to travel. Each were asked to type in the word "chicken" into their search engines. The Conservative was provided a list that included "chicken fried steak." The Liberal was provided "organic, free-range chicken," and the Moderates' search offered up advertisements to "travel to Kentucky."

If the very information we receive is skewed based on algorithms that are designed to reaffirm what we already believe, how can we ever develop a balanced viewpoint? One of the most dangerous aspects to social media is that we are communicating with people who are only like we are. People that have similar opinions and perspectives. The information we receive from them often validates our own perspectives. People who "like" the photos we like, who "retweet" the ideas we agree with, and who "share" cute dog videos similar to the ones we do on social media. It can all become a self replicating loop feeding similar content and ideologies.

Obtaining unskewed information in today's world is very challenging. When we receive information based on proclivities rather than realities, it may lead to a dangerous confirmation bias that promotes a herd mentality and inspires looking for support for conclusions we have already made, rather than objectively looking at the world as it truly exists.

Rather than first give you an opinion of where we are headed, I will begin by starting with where we have already been. The future is unknowable, the past is unchangeable. Before arguing what new strategy you should consider for the future, let's be sure we are on the same page as to what has already occurred and the underlying reasons why. From there, a new strategy will be revealed.

THE EVERYTHING BUBBLE

*"I can't afford a vacation so I'm just going to drink until I
don't know where I am"*

Dean Martin

Stocks Are Significantly Overvalued And In A BUBBLE

A bubble can be defined as an *extended period of time where
asset values are significantly higher than their historical norms.*
So how do we know if we are in a bubble or not? Believe it or
not, just like medical tests that tell us if our numbers are in a
healthy range, there are also ways to measure whether assets are
undervalued, fairly valued, or overvalued. Investing is actually
not very complicated. Everything you need to know about
investing you probably learned at a very young age. *Buy low and
sell high.*

Where the complexity can arise is in deciphering what is low
and what is high. This mandate would be a lot easier to follow
if we knew how to more accurately measure value. The reality
is that most average investors do the exact opposite. They buy
when things are high and sell when they are low.

Warren Buffett is among the most famous investors in the
world. He has a story that he tells about investing that goes the
following way. "In the Buffett household we love hamburgers.
We will be eating hamburgers in the Buffett household for the rest

of our lives. When the price of a hamburger is high, we sing the blues because we won't be able to afford as many hamburgers. And, when the price of a hamburger is low we sing for joy, since when that occurs we can afford even more hamburgers." He then goes on to say the following: "I find that most people are the exact same way when it comes to almost everything, *except* for the stock market. For some reason when stocks are *high* people want to buy them and when stocks are *low* is when most people want to sell. I prefer cheap hamburgers and will do my best to sell when prices are high and buy when prices are low."

Wouldn't it be great to be able to invest like Warren Buffett? To *know* if things are high or low? To see bubbles for what they are and get out of them before they pop right in our face and get stuck all over us?

If you are a long-term buy and hold investor it's imperative to understand the key to your overall success will be the *value* at which you acquire assets. When you buy assets that are undervalued and hold them for a long time, your portfolio performance will be very good. If you buy and hold assets that are overvalued, your long term gains will be poor.

Buffett has another saying that further makes this point. He calls it the *greater fool theory of investing.* He suggests; "You can make money holding overvalued assets. You just need to find a bigger fool down the road willing to pay more than you did."

Warren Buffett's wisdom can actually help you *right now*. He has a preferred metric he uses to measure the overall value of the stock market at any given time. It's become so famous that many people call it the Warren Buffett Indicator. In a 2001 interview with Fortune Magazine, Warren Buffett is quoted as saying "The best single measure of where stock valuations are at any moment is the Market Cap/GDP Ratio." The ratio compares how much cash is invested in the stock market at any given time, and then compares it to overall GDP.

Buffett went on to say that investors can get caught up in the moment and chase returns. Long term value is best determined by price. The best way for Warren Buffet to know if the *price* of the overall market was high or low was to compare total cash invested in the market to GDP. Looking at this ratio over time and the history of our stock markets produced the following conclusions by Buffett:

When the total amount of money in the stock market is between 70-90% of GDP our equity markets are *fairly valued.* When the total amount of money in the market is below 50% of GDP the equity market is **significantly undervalued.** When the amount of cash in the equity market is above 115% the market is **significantly overvalued.**

Image 8		
Ratio = Total Market Cap / GDP	Valuation	
Ratio < 50%	Significantly Undervalued	**Where is it now?**
50% < Ratio < 75%	Modestly Undervalued	
75% < Ratio < 90%	**Fair Valued**	CALCULATE
90% < Ratio < 115%	Modestly Overvalued	
Ratio > 115%	Significantly Overvalued	

Do the calculation yourself. Go to www.goldisabetterway.com

The following chart will highlight this metric. Notice that when this ratio is very high like it was in 1929, 2000 and in 2008 markets were overvalued and thereafter suffered major losses. Notice as well, at the times when this ratio was lowest, the long term performance of the overall equity market was excellent.

Remember the Dot Com Bubble? Technology stocks were so hot that if they had a 'dotcom' on the end of their name their stock would fly through the roof. These were companies that had huge valuations but actually *produced* very little. These tech darlings of the time were built on promise and hope, not on actual revenues. There was a lot of cash invested in these companies with very little real production or revenue. Thus the very high ratio.

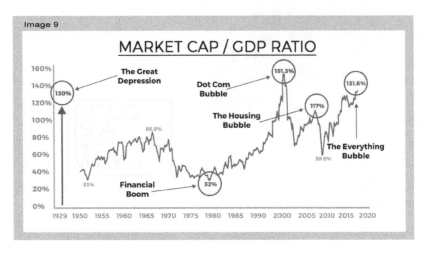

The *lowest* this ratio ever measured was back in 1982. If you remember this time you will recall that interest rates hit highs of 20%. With interest rates this high, money flowed out of risky investments like stocks and into fixed and safer investments like certificates of deposit, bank accounts and government treasuries. Stocks would hereafter go on an 18-year bull run. They were significantly *undervalued* in 1982. Investors that bought into the stock market in 1982 were rewarded with more than 10 times returns over the next 18 years.

The Warren Buffett indicator makes logical sense when examined against these historical periods. Where is that ratio today and what might it tell us? Today this ratio sits at 149.6%.

By this measurement, the overall stock market today is *significantly overvalued* and has only been this overvalued one other time in history. Remember, Warren Buffett believes this is the very most important metric we can pay attention to and it's *screaming* alarm bells. Incidentally, as of this writing, Warren Buffett has over $115 Billion sitting in a cash position. This

Ratio = Total Market Cap / GDP	Valuation	Where is it now?
Ratio < 50%	Significantly Undervalued	
50% < Ratio < 75%	Modestly Undervalued	CALCULATE
75% < Ratio < 90%	Fair Valued	
90% < Ratio < 115%	Modestly Overvalued	As of 01/01/2018
		149.19%
Ratio > 115%	Significantly Overvalued	Significantly Overvalued

Do the calculation yourself. Go to www.goldisabetterway.com

amounts to more than 50% of his investable portfolio. Buffet follows his own advice.

To be clear this is not to say that the market cannot go higher from here. There were a lot of people who got rich in a hurry during the dot-com boom as they played the market and invested in overvalued companies while they were going higher. In 1999 Warren Buffett himself missed much of the last final euphoric burst of the market. He got out 12% below all-time highs. He missed the last bit of the party. He also missed all of the pain when equity markets collapsed in early 2000. Warren Buffett thereafter bought what he liked at a major discount after stocks collapsed.

In February 2007, Warren Buffett followed this ratio again and moved out of the markets leaving roughly 40% his portfolio in a cash position. Markets would not hit their peak of 14% higher until eight months later October 2007. Buffet missed the last move higher.

You may remember that after the financial crisis hit in earnest in 2008, Warren Buffett was one of the few people with dry powder. He bailed out Bank of America and bought their stock at pennies on the dollar. He bailed out Goldman Sachs at a dramatic discount, and was instrumental in propping up AIG Insurance. Buffet arguably helped keep the financial markets from sinking into the abyss by having cash available on the sidelines to bring to the rescue.

Perhaps this time Buffet is wrong and the markets will just continue higher indefinitely? At the moment the financial markets would seem to be mocking Buffet's wisdom as they continue to rise steadily. Since moving a large portion of his portfolio to cash in February 2017, Buffett has missed out on the last 15% move higher as stocks have surged to all-time highs.

Or maybe he has a different strategy. Buffett is not a sprinter trying to glean maximum returns at all times. He understands that more risk means more pain when markets turn. He is a value investor. He invests like a marathon runner, not a sprinter. While most investors are running full steam ahead with the *all in* strategy Wall Street espouses, Buffet is pacing himself. He knows that while other investors may rush out and take a lead, he will likely glide right past them when their *all in, all the time* strategies run out of steam. Warren Buffet understands **value**.

If your strategy is to keep running full steam ahead and find a bigger fool to sell to down the road, you may want to be sure there are some left because there is a chance that if you wait too long, that fool could be you.

CAPE Shiller - Another Way To Way To Measure Price

As investors we are counting on the future earnings and profits of the companies we invest in. This is why earnings are the lifeblood of corporate America. Price to Earnings (P/E) Ratios are a good way to look at the *price* of a company's stock.

Robert Shiller is a Yale economist who developed what has become the most adopted measure of P/E ratios for the overall market. Rather than take the future predicted earnings Wall Street has famously manipulated, Shiller came up with a more consistent metric. It looks at the last 10 years of earnings and adjusts them for inflation to come up with an overall price for the stock market. His P/E ratio has been widely accepted to be the most accurate long term metric to determine overall value of the market at any given time. It is specifically known as the CAPE Shiller (Cyclically Adjusted Price to Earnings) and the graph below demonstrates its historical measurements.

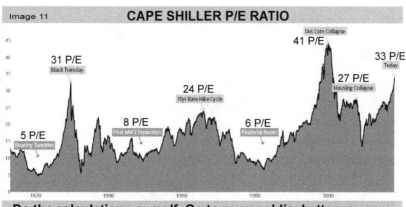

The *average* historical CAPE Shiller P/E ratio for the stock market is roughly 17 times earnings. When the P/E ratio is significantly below this multiple it's a great indication that the market is undervalued. Long term investors who have put their money into the market when P/E ratios are below 10 have seen tremendous long term performance. Alternatively investors who buy and hold when P/E ratio's are above 24 experience poor long term performance.

Notice that those who invest when multiples are low go on to see exceptional long term gains. Investors that hold equities when P/E multiples are high go on to see poor long term gains. If you were able to invest in June 1982, at the beginning the Reagan era financial boom, when P/E multiples were only 6 times earnings, your long term gains were exceptional as the market went on a 18-year bull run thereafter.

Think of P/E ratio as price. When the P/E multiple is high, the price is high, and when low, the price is low. Never forget that the key to investing is to *buy low* and *sell high.*

Image 12

P/E RATIO	FIVE YEAR AVERAGE RETURN
Below 10	Excellent (Plus 15% Annual Avg)
14 - 18	Average (7% Annual Avg)
Above 24	Poor (Minus 15% Annual Avg)

Where is it now?

CALCULATE

As of 01/01/2018

33PE

See where it is now! Go to www.goldisabetterway.com

The CAPE Shiller P/E ratio for the market currently is at 33 times earnings. Based on this ratio the market is nearly 100% higher than historical long term norms. Can you afford to lose half your money if valuations return to their historical norms? This 50% reversion to the mean would put CAPE Shiller P/E multiples closer to their historical averages.

Revenues vs. Profits

Another way to look at price is by comparing stock prices to *revenues*. Today there are 28 companies that currently trade at more than 10X revenues!! Coincidentally, the exact same number of companies that traded above 10 times revenues at the peak of dot com boom. Facebook currently trades at 15X revenues. Think about what this means. If Facebook had zero costs of goods sold (virtually impossible), and zero employees (they have 25,000), never paid any taxes (really hard to do), and spent zero dollars on Research and Development (R&D), it would take 15 years of payments of *100% of revenues* in order to get investment dollars out to breakeven.

Let's look at this in a slightly different way. Suppose I own a pizza shop. I pay rent, utilities, employee payroll, vendors who provide me with ingredients for my food and other fixed expenses of running the pizza shop. The shop also has marketing and other expenses. Let's say the shop is very successful. It brings in $1,200,000 per year in revenues against costs of only $800,000. That's $400,000 of actual *earnings* or profit per year.

Not a bad business! But is it worth 15 times revenues? That would mean the pizza shop is worth $18,000,000 when the store is only providing $400,000 of profit.

Would you buy a pizza shop for $18M when it took in a profit of $400,000 per year? If you did it would take you 45 years of taking *every penny of the profit* to get your $18M back. You wouldn't even begin to make a profit until the 46th year. Sounds outrageous right? Anyone owning Facebook is making this similar bargain right now.

Do you own stock in Netflix? Most people do. If you do you are investing in a company that is trading at 13 times revenues and 218 times earnings. If Netflix doesn't grow from here it would take 218 years just to get your money back as an investor.

Do you own Amazon stock? Most people do. Those investors will need to wait 355 years, if Amazon doesn't grow, to get their money back.

Do you own shares of Google? Most people do. If so, you'll only have to wait 40 years to get your money back if Google doesn't continue to grow.

Company	P/E Ratio	Revenue	Market Cap	Revenue
Facebook	36	$36.8B	$552B	15x
Amazon	355	$136B	$675B	5x
Netflix	218	$8.8B	$118B	13x
Google	40	$89.46B	$821B	9x

The problem is that almost every investor in today's markets owns these outrageously expensive companies either directly or within Mutual Funds and Exchange Traded Funds (ETF's).

Besides being richly valued these companies have another thing in common. Not one of them pays a dividend. The only reason to own these stocks is to be able to sell them for a higher share price to someone else. When valuations revert towards their mean, as they always have in history, investors who own them will be left holding the bag.

This Time Is Different...

Maybe we are in a new environment where price no longer matters? Kenneth Rogoff, the famous American Economist and Professor of Economics at Harvard University, along with his co-writer Carmen Reinhart, dedicated an in-depth study to this exact question. They wrote an entire 512 page book to attempt to answer this topic. *This Time Is Different, Eight Centuries of Financial Folly* was released in 2009 and covers financial crises that have occurred over the last 800 years.

What did they find in this comprehensive study? No matter how different the latest financial hysteria or crisis appears, there are always remarkable similarities with the past throughout history. Investors repeatedly overlook price in an effort to justify bubbles. Rogoff and Reinhart's conclusion? **It's never different.**

The Buffet Indicator is at 149.6%. The CAPE Shiller is at 33 times earnings. Many companies are trading over 10x revenues. These statistics tell us that the *price* to own equities is incredibly high at the moment. Holding assets that are overpriced has never been a great long term strategy. Unless of course, this time is different.

5 THE BOND BUBBLE BLUES

"Can't play the blues no more, done found happiness"

B.B. King

Bonds Are Dramatically Overvalued

When we invest in a *bond* we are becoming a *lender*. We can lend our money to corporations in the form of Corporate Bonds, or we can lend our money to the government in the form of Treasury Bonds. What is the best way to measure if bonds are undervalued or overvalued?

The main underlying fundamentals for stocks are *earnings and profit*. The main underlying fundamental for bonds are *interest rates*. The term "price" when referring to a bond can be confusing. The *higher* the yield or interest rate the *lower* the price. Conversely when interest rates are lower, bond prices are higher. A bond that pays a 6% coupon rate for example, has a lower price than a bond that pays a coupon rate of only 3%.

But what is *normal* or average? The historical average for the *prime* interest rate is 7%. The prime rate is the rate at which banks lend to the public, and is most closely correlated to the 30 Year Treasury Note, the rate that the government pays its long term creditors. What is most important to recognize is that interest rates are near historical lows. The prime rate has averaged roughly 3% over the last decade, nowhere near the 7% historically average.

With these low levels of yield, bonds have rarely been more expensive. There has never been a better time in history to be a borrower! What is good for the borrower who gets to acquire money virtually for free, is bad for the lender as the *price* to lend has never been steeper. Interest rates at these historically low levels leave bondholders in the unenviable position of lending money that yields virtually no return.

We are on a 37-year bull run in interest rates. The Fed Funds Rate has continued to come down over time from roughly 20% in 1981 to 1% today. It seems obvious that there are only two ways for rates to go from here as there is not much room to go lower. They can either go sideways or higher.

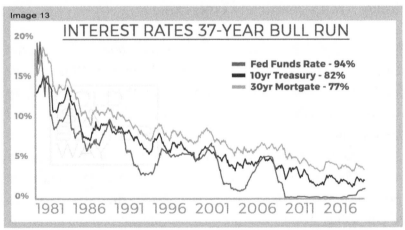

While negative interest rates actually exist on about $10 Trillion of sovereign and corporate debt around the globe currently, the financial system cannot function with ongoing negative interest rates. If we go into negative interest rates in the United States it will be a signal that The Federal Reserve has lost all credibility and that our economy is in serious trouble. Gold would likely soar to previously unimaginable levels in that scenario.

Alan Greenspan, our former Fed Chairman has been sounding alarm bells that the bond market is in a bubble and on the verge of popping. He suggests that the greatest risks to the world economy are interest rates that surge higher from these levels. He argues that when this occurs we are headed for serious *stagflation*, defined as an extended period of time of low GDP growth alongside an inflation in prices.

Greenspan points out it could look very much like the late 1970's where the economy went through serious recessions. During this time inflation spiked dramatically and low GDP growth was persistent. Gold skyrocketed from $150 per ounce in 1977 to $800 per ounce by 1980 as interest rates surged higher. Notice as interest rates went higher from 1977 to 1980, bonds lost value and gold soared.

Image 14

10YR TREASURY				GOLD			
START	END	VALUE	AVG YIELD	START	END	CHANGE	%CHANGE
7.43	10.82	$68,669.13	8.55%	$148.30	$835.00	$686.70	463.05%

$85,774.57 $563,047.88

INVESTMENT   START 04/01/1977
$ 100,000   END 01/18/1980

Do the calculation yourself. Go to www.goldisabetterway.com

What makes all of this even scarier according to Greenspan is, "There are no longer any financial professionals on Wall Street who have lived through a rising interest rate environment. The folks on Wall Street only know rates that head south, not north." Greenspan highlights that interest rate cycles can last for a long time. This current 37-year cycle of lower interest rates was preceded by a 22 year cycle from 1959 to 1981, when the Fed Funds Rate soared from under 2% to over 20%. Rates that zoom higher are not only bad for bondholders but can also punish equity investors as well.

Greenspan predicts that this 37-year downward cycle will reverse over the next few years and when it does it will likely be very painful for investors. According to Greenspan, "The bond market is extremely overvalued and in big bubble."

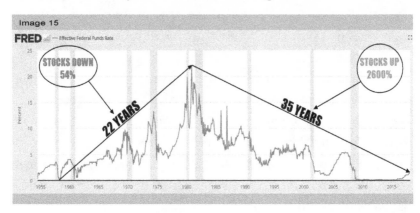

This is the MASSIVE problem facing investors today! *Both* stocks and bonds are significantly higher than their historical norms. They are *both* expensive *at the same time*. So holding stocks and bonds as *diversification* for the portfolio as a strategy may make less sense than ever before since all this paper is more correlated than ever. The Wall Street way, which almost every investor is following, may be the worst strategy as all of this occurs.

If stocks and bonds are both the most expensive they've ever been, and very correlated due to low interest rates, where should investors look to diversify? I believe the answer is **gold**.

6 THE FOUNDATION

"If you don't have time do it right, when will you have time to do it over?"

John Wooden

Gold Is Undervalued

The entire monetary system has been built on the foundation of gold. The United States owns the most physical gold in the world and holds roughly 8,000 tons. Germany owns roughly 3,500 tons of gold. The International Monetary Fund (IMF), Italy and France possess roughly 2,500 tons each. The amount of gold that China holds is a subject of great debate. Officially they report holdings of 1,900 tons. However, insiders estimate that total amount could be more than twice as large, and is continuing to grow annually. Russia reports holdings of 1,715 tons. Every major country in the world keeps vaults of physical gold.

These statistics beg a simple question: why physical gold? If gold is as useless as Wall Street would have us believe, why does every major superpower and established country in the world keep it?

The answer is simple: *he who has the gold makes the rules.* That is why we keep it, Russia is hoarding it and China is accumulating more. Gold is integral to the world's monetary system. These facts beg an important question. If gold is good for major governments to own, why is gold a bad thing for you to own?

If you've followed gold prices you may know that in 2011 they hit an all time high of $1,924 per ounce. As of January 1st, 2018, the price of gold is $1,296 per ounce. The first argument to make supporting the attractive price level of gold is one of timing. While almost every financial asset is up at or near all-time highs and far above their historical norms, gold is down nearly 40% from all time highs. For many "smart money" investors this fact alone is enough to be rotating out of equities or bonds and into gold. Remember, the key is to *buy low and sell high.*

However, my argument goes much deeper than that. It's not enough to say gold is currently down in price and therefore undervalued, but rather to make the case as to exactly why. My aim is to show you how you can evaluate this for yourself. Gold is not only undervalued. I believe gold will outperform paper assets in a large way in the coming years.

Notice that the price of gold has increased in value 14 of the last 17 years. Not only in U.S. Dollars, but *every major currency in the world,* (see Image 16). This surprises most people. Why has this occurred?

Since the turn of the century virtually every major government has undertaken programs of money printing, currency devaluation and excessive deficit spending. Gold should continue to rise in value in all currencies undertaking these programs, so long as this trend continues.

The average annual increase in the price of gold in U.S. Dollars since the year 2002 has been 11.1% per year. By contrast, the average annual increase in the Dow Jones during that same exact span has been 6.1%. These numbers are more glaringly surprising when considering gold is down over $650 per ounce and the Dow Jones has never been higher.

World Gold Prices (%)

Image 16

YEAR	USD	CNY	EUR	GBP	INR	JPY
2002	+ 24.6	+ 24.6	+ 5.9	+ 13.0	+ 23.8	+ 12.0
2003	+ 19.7	+ 19.7	+ 0.5	+ 8.6	+ 13.6	+ 7.7
2004	+ 5.3	+ 5.3	- 2.7	- 2.3	+ 0.6	+ 0.7
2005	+ 20.0	+ 17.0	+ 36.8	+ 33.0	+ 24.2	+ 37.6
2006	+ 23.0	+ 19.1	+ 10.6	+ 8.1	+ 20.9	+ 23.0
2007	+ 30.9	+ 23.6	+ 18.4	+ 29.2	+ 16.5	+ 22.9
2008	+ 5.6	- 2.4	+ 10.5	+ 43.2	+ 28.8	- 14.4
2009	+ 23.4	+ 23.6	+ 20.7	+ 12.7	+ 19.3	+ 26.8
2010	+ 29.5	+ 24.9	+ 38.8	+ 34.3	+ 23.7	+ 13.0
2011	+ 10.1	+ 5.9	+ 14.2	+ 10.5	+ 31.6	+ 4.5
2012	+ 7.0	+ 6.2	+ 4.9	+ 2.2	+ 10.3	+ 20.7
2013	- 28.3	- 30.2	- 31.2	- 29.4	- 18.7	- 12.8
2014	- 1.5	+ 1.2	+ 12.1	+ 5.0	+ 0.8	+ 12.3
2015	- 10.4	- 6.2	- 0.3	- 5.2	- 5.9	- 10.1
2016	+ 9.1	+ 16.8	+ 12.4	+ 30.2	+ 11.9	+ 5.8
2017	+ 13.6	+ 3.0	- 3.9	- 0.4	+ 2.2	+ 4.5
AVERAGE	+ 11.1	+ 9.4	+ 9.2	+ 12.0	+ 12.7	+ 9.7

See this chart real time. Go to www.goldisabetterway.com

But what impacts the price of gold? Wall Street would prefer to think of gold as a barbarous relic. They argue that gold has no rhyme or reason, and its future performance is impossible to predict. Critics point out that gold doesn't do anything, it just sits there and doesn't provide any return. Those arguing against owning gold will drive home the point that one must be crazy to own gold. They say gold is for people who are conspiracy theorists and are worried about the end of the world. Successfully branding gold in this negative way has allowed Wall Street critics to keep its paper laden monopoly humming right along.

The Four Pillars

Gold is a chameleon and an asset investors flock to at different times. There are four main pillars that can move the price of gold higher or lower at various times. These various underlying drivers can make gold difficult to predict at certain times.

1. *Financial Crisis / Military Conflict:*
   Investors rush to the safe haven of precious metals in times of economic uncertainty. This is the fundamental most people associate with gold and why gold is often misperceived as a bearish asset. For example, in the aftermath of the financial crisis in 2008 gold would rise from $700 per ounce to over $1,900 per ounce in just three years. Investment capital flowed out of *risk on* assets like the stock market and into gold during this time.

2. *Inflationary Pressures:*
   Gold rises in value as paper currencies devalue. This has occurred regularly since the turn of the century in every major currency in the world and why gold is up more than five times from its $250 per ounce level in 2000. During runaway inflation from 1977 to 1980, gold rose dramatically from $150 per ounce to $800 per ounce as interest rates and inflationary pressures surged higher. As inflationary pressures increased in the early 2000's, The Federal Reserve would raise interest rates from 1% to 5.5%. During this time gold would outperform both stocks and bonds and nearly double in price.

3. *Government Debt & Deficits:*
   Currencies strengthen when debt levels decrease and weaken as debt and deficits increase. For example, gold would lose 40% of its value from 1996 to 2000 as the United States Government was in budget surplus and paid down the national debt.

4. *Equity Market Enthusiasm:*

Because gold is perceived as a bearish asset by many investors, when the animal spirits of the market for risk grow, gold can lose appeal as other investments are more exciting. When investors have a *risk on* mindset more money flows to equities and gold will often sell off. When equity market confidence diminishes and investors become more fearful, gold often gets a bid.

Image 17

	Financial/Military Crisis High Risk / Low Risk	Inflationary Pressures High / Low	Government Debt Deficits Rising / Lowering	Equity Market Confidence Low / High
10				
9				
8				
7				
6				
5				
4				
3				
2				
1				
0				

Do the calculation yourself. Go to www.goldisabetterway.com

The four pillars that impact the price of gold can either be a headwind or tailwind depending on timing and sentiment. For the first time in a decade it appears that each pillar may be perfectly aligned for a higher gold price at the same time. The stock market is at all time highs with extreme valuations and the risks for investors are heavily inflated. Military conflicts in the Middle East are turning into hot wars and the rhetoric between our political leaders has intensified. Interest rates are rising, indicating inflationary pressures. Government debt and deficits are exploding. Equity market enthusiasm is a fickle friend. While currently at euphoric extremes, that mood assuredly cannot continue forever.

GOLDEN NUGGET #3

Things that make you go "Hmmm..."

What if the total return of the Dow over the next 10 years was 0%? Would you change your strategy?

Virtually every investor has been programmed to believe that the best way to invest is to buy and hold stocks. But what if you knew that the total return of the stock market would be 0% over the next 10 years? Impossible, right? Believe it or not this is more common than you may think - from 1971 to 1980 to total return of the Dow was -3%.

Do the calculation yourself. Go to www.goldisabetterway.com

From 2000 to 2010 the total return of the Dow was -8%.

Do the calculation yourself. Go to www.goldisabetterway.com

Three of the last *five* decades, the Dow boomed. *Two* of the last *five* decades, the Dow produced *negative returns*. Perhaps we are beginning another 10 year span where the Dow returns nothing. Many experts are predicting just that.

7   PRIMARY PILLAR

"I'm so deep in debt that my goal in life is to get back to broke"

Woody Allan

Future Gold Price? Government Debt And Deficits Are The Key

Stock analysts can look at *book value, cash flow, earnings, dividends, debt service*, and other hard numbers that allow for a forecasting of future value. Stocks have identifiable *fundamentals*. Bond investors can look at *interest rates, credit ratings, and inflation expectations*. Bonds also have fundamentals.

But what are the fundamentals of gold? Gold performs for different reasons at different times. However, there is one long-term fundamental that most impacts the future price of gold: *rising government debt and deficits*.

While we are no longer on a gold standard, gold is still the standard by which our currency is measured because gold is priced in dollars. To understand the fundamentals of gold, simply understand the fundamentals of the dollar. The fundamentals of the dollar are actually *written* on every bill ever issued. Printed on every dollar bill are three words: *Federal Reserve Note*. Understanding these words will better help us understand the fundamentals of the bill they are printed on.

Image 20

A *note* can be defined as a debt, an obligation, or a promise. Therefore the paper currency we carry in our pockets is effectively a *promise* of the Federal Reserve. Remember, it's a promise that at one time was backed by gold.

Since the dollar is no longer backed by gold, what then backs the dollar today? Many would argue that the dollar is not backed by anything. Many would say that as a *fiat currency* there is nothing backing the dollar. I don't agree with this conclusion. Nor would our Federal Reserve.

If you asked Janet Yellen, our former Federal Reserve Chairwoman, she would say that the dollar is backed by the *full faith and credit of the United States*. Therefore, the dollar is backed by *faith in our country* and our country's *credit rating*.

The factors that impact *faith* are subjective and debatable. The underlying factors determining *credit worthiness* are more objective and measurable.

What are the fundamentals of our country's credit rating that determine the strength of our currency? The fundamentals of *any* country's currency and credit rating have three main components. These are fundamentals that can be measured and are considered hard data. There are also forecasts like GDP growth and future productivity forecasts that are considered soft data.

The three main fundamentals of the dollar are:

1. **Money Supply:** *Adding* to the supply of something *dilutes* its value. *Subtracting* from the supply of something *increases* its value.
2. **Interest Rates:** When interest rates are high, the cost to borrow a dollar is more expensive. When interest rates are low, the costs to borrow a dollar is less expensive.
3. **Ability To Service National Debt:** When debt levels are low, a country is better suited to repay. When debt levels are high, a country is less suited to be able to repay.

The United States has *tripled* the money supply over the past 10 years, thereby diluting the dollar's value. Interest rates have never been lower and therefore borrowing a dollar has never been cheaper. Our National Debt has increased 150% in the last decade, from $8 Trillion to over $20 Trillion today, indicating that our ability to service debt is now far worse, not better.

The three main fundamentals of the dollar are all *screaming* that the dollar has been *devalued* and should therefore be weakening. Gold, by contrast, should be rising in price. Which is why it may not surprise you to learn that in the last 10 years, **gold is up 55%.** This small price movement higher, however, does not reflect the *massive devaluation* and current position of the U.S. Dollar

Gold vs. National Debt

There has been a direct correlation with the amount of our country's national debt and the price of gold over the past 30 years. From 1987 to 2002 our national debt averaged $3.4 Trillion dollars and the price of gold averaged roughly $340 per ounce. From 1996 to 2000, as we paid down our national debt from $4 Trillion to $2.7 Trillion, the price of gold dropped from $400 per ounce to $270 per ounce. From 2001 to 2011, as our national

73

debt rose from $3 Trillion to $15 Trillion, the price of gold surged from $300 per ounce to $1,500 per ounce.

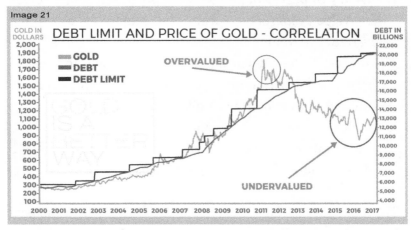

Image 21

This correlation is known as the Gold To National Debt Ratio. According to this metric, in 2011 when gold spiked to over $1900 per ounce while we were $15 Trillion in debt, the price of gold was *overvalued*. Conversely, with our national debt at over $20 Trillion and the price of gold at $1,300, gold is currently **undervalued** by over $700 per ounce.

Debt To GDP Ratio

In the aforementioned book, *This Time Is Different*, Rogoff and Reinhart focus on this very point. Their conclusion was that a country's economic growth declines dramatically when a country's level of public debt rises relative to Gross Domestic Product. Rogoff warns, "There is no question that the most significant vulnerability as we emerge from recession is soaring government debt. It's very likely that will trigger the next crisis as government debts have been stretched so wide." Their research found that GDP averages between 3-4% when the public debt to GDP ratio is below 90%. However, when that ratio exceeds 90%, average growth can collapse to as low as 2%. The debt to GDP ratio of the United States currently sits at 103%.

Image 22

Where is it now?

CALCULATE

As of 01/30/2018

103%

DEBT

$20,493,107,046,027

GDP

$19,738,890,000.00

See where it's at today. Go to www.goldisabetterway.com

Debt Went Up But Gold Came Down... What Happened?!

Gold prices hit a high of $1,924 per ounce in 2011. If you acquired gold at these levels you have been wildly disappointed and may be frustrated as the price of gold has dropped. Why has gold come down at all in the face of the United States printing $4.5 Trillion in new money supply and coupled with a National Debt now north of $20 Trillion that continues to surge higher?

From 2012 through 2015 U.S. debt rose from $16 Trillion to over $18 Trillion. That is an increase of over $2 Trillion in additional debt over three years, and yet gold dropped from over $1,900 per ounce all the way down to $1,050 per ounce by the end of 2015. This move lower has frustrated gold bugs who watch debt levels as the only indicator for the price of gold.

While overall level of national debt is important, what really needs to be considered is a country's *ability to service their debt.* It is this one thing that most impacts the credit rating and the overall strength or weakness of country's currency. This *debt affordability* is a primary fundamental of our country's credit rating, and therefore the long term indicator of the future strength or weakness of the dollar.

You Want To Borrow $100,000? No Problem!

Let's use an example to make the point. Suppose you borrowed $100,000 from a bank and at an annual interest rate of 5%. It would cost $5,000 in annual interest payments to *service the interest* on this loan each year.

Let's say a year goes by and the bank comes with good news. They've lowered interest rates to 2.5% and you can refinance your loan. This allows for a 50% decrease in the costs to service this loan. At a 2.5% interest rate it will only cost $2,500 per year to now service the loan. Interest rates going lower allowed for a lower interest payment. The additional $2,500 saved can now be used to pay down the principle on the loan or spent elsewhere on discretionary spending.

There's also another option; you could borrow another $100,000 and still pay the same $5,000 in annual interest payments. Borrow double the money and pay the same amount - how do you say no to that? So, you borrow an extra $100,000, bringing your principal amount to $200,000.

This is a great deal, until it isn't. What happens when the bank comes back later and tells you that interest rates have gone back up to 5%? Now you have a bit of a problem. Your total debt is $200,000. The annual interest payments at 5% will now cost you $10,000 per year.

Interest rates going *lower* allowed you to lower your debt service and technically *strengthen* your credit rating. Interest rates going *higher* have the opposite effect. Interest rates going higher will *weaken* your credit rating as more dollars must be allocated to interest payments.

This is exactly what has happened to U.S. debt and why gold went down from 2012 through 2015. As interest rates went lower *our ability to service our debt strengthened, allowing our country's underlying credit rating to effectively get stronger even* *though we were adding to the overall debt.* We have doubled the national debt over the past decade, and yet we pay roughly the same amount today in interest payments as we did in 2008.

This is why gold came down in value: **it's all about the costs!** When costs drive higher like they did from 2002 to 2011, the price of gold rises. When costs to service debt come down like they did from 2012 to 2015, the price of gold declines as the dollar strengthens.

Future Gold Price? It's All About The Costs

YEAR	TOTAL NATIONAL DEBT	COST TO SERVICE/ NATION DEBT	PRICE OF GOLD	INCREASE/ DECREASE
2003	$6,783,231,062,743	$318,148,529,151.51	$417	+19.79%
2004	$7,379,052,696,330	$321,566,323,971.29	$435	+5.3%
2005	$7,932,709,661,723	$352,350,252,507.90	$513	+20.00%
2006	$8,506,973,899,215	$405,872,109,315.83	$635	+23.04%
2007	$9,007,653,372,262	$429,977,998,108.20	$836	+30.92
2008	$10,024,724,896,912	$451,154,049,950.63	$869	+5.6%
2009	$11,909,829,003,891	$383,071,060,815.42	$1087	+23.43%
2010	$13,561,623,030,891	$413,954,825,362.17	$1420	+29.54%
2011	$14,790,340,328,557	$454,393,280,417.03	$1531	+8.72
2012	$16,066,241,407,385	$359,796,008,919.49	$1664	+7.08
2013	$16,738,183,526,697	$415,688,781,248.40	$1204	-28.32%
2014	$17,824,071,380,733	$430,812,121,372.05	$1199	-1.42%
2015	$18,150,617,666,484	$402,435,356,075.49	$1060	-10.42%
2016	$19,573,762,877,248	$432,649,652,901.12	$1142	+9.10%
2017	$20,245,872,760,229	$458,542,287,311.80	$1257	+9.72%
2018	$21.1T (est)	$550B (est)	?	?
2019	$22.3T (est)	$670B (est)	?	?
2020	$24.1T (est)	$750B (est)	?	?

We are now $20 Trillion in debt and The Fed is *raising* interest rates. Since 2016, The Fed has raised interest rates five times. As they have done this, the cost to service our national debt has driven higher and the price of gold has gone from $1,050 per ounce to $1,295 per ounce.

Looking at the following chart, one can see how the costs to service our debt have moved laterally over the last 30 years while our debt has continued to surge over time. We have been able to continually increase the total amount of debt we have taken on without impacting our overall costs because we have continued to refinance our debt at lower interest rates.

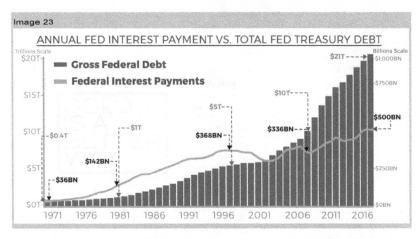

This is a ponzi scheme that cannot continue forever. As The Fed continues to hike interest rates and unwind their balance sheet over the next several years the costs to service our national debt will continue to drive higher.

According to the Congressional Budget Office (CBO) the cost to service our national debt could *double* over the next five years. These costs will rise from $460 Billion in 2017 to over $800 Billion in 2021. This estimate is *without adding anything to the national debt total.* The tax cut passed in December 2017 will add a *minimum* of $1.5 Trillion in debt over the next ten years which hasn't been factored into this equation about future debt affordability. The real costs to service debt could be even higher than these CBO projections. Debt service will hit $1 Trillion annually within the next seven years.

Interest rates going higher into an already stratospheric debt are a stinging one-two punch that will guarantee a much higher cost to service debt over time. The fact that we have expanding and not contracting budget deficits only further exacerbates the fragile situation. As our costs to service debt go higher, I expect the price of gold to move dramatically higher as well.

This is the primary reason I believe you will see the price of gold above $2,500 per ounce within the next four years. The costs to service our National Debt will likely double during this time. I believe the price of gold will, at a minimum, double as this occurs.

8   CHOICES

"I don't lose, I let other people win"

Rodney Dangerfield

The Stats Don't Lie

The title of this book is *Gold Is a Better Way.* I don't say gold is good or bad, or that gold is the only way. My assertion is that gold is *better*. Better for who? Better than what? Better than virtually all of the other long term investment options available at the moment. Gold has been a better way for a very long time.

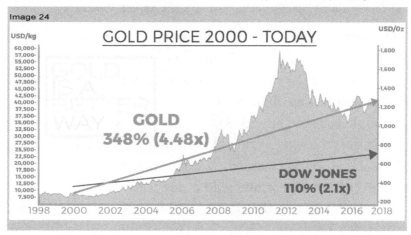

The Dow Jones traded at 11,722 points on January 14th, 2000. As of January 1st, 2018 the Dow closed at 24,720, for an increase of 110% over 17 years. On that same date 17 years ago gold was $284 per ounce. In the period its taken the Dow Jones to go up 110%, (2.1X), the price of gold has gone up 348%, (4.48X).

This direct comparison between gold and the Dow Jones can be slightly misleading. Gold is priced in dollars. The Dow Jones is an index and is measured in points. Additionally, gold does not pay a dividend and therefore its sum total is a more direct calculation. Long term investors in the equity markets may receive the benefits of dividends that get reinvested and then compounded over time. This calculation is called *total return.*

To offer a fair comparison we must consider the total return of the market versus the total return of gold.

Image 25

DOW JONES			GOLD			
START	END	% CHANGE	START	END	CHANGE	%CHANGE
11,722.98	24,719.22	110.86%	$283.30	$1,291.00	$1,007.70	355.70%

** Total return: $318,798.94

$210,861.23 $455,700.67

	INVESTMENT	START	01/14/2000
	$ 100,000	END	01/01/2018

Do the calculation yourself. Go to www.goldisabetterway.com

The **total return** of the Dow Jones since 2000 through 2017 is 218%. Gold is up 355% in the same period. If you invested $100,000 in the Dow Jones in January 2000 and never touched it, and allowed your dividends to compound, on January 1st 2018 you would have roughly $318,000. That same $100,000 invested in gold over the same period of time would be worth $455,000. This comparison is measured at a time when the stock market **has never been higher and gold is down 40%.**

In a race between the equity markets and gold, where the markets have been running at record pace for the last decade, and gold has been left for dead as an asset that Wall Street tells you not to own, gold's performance has kicked the daylights out of the stock market.

Perhaps gold's performance will be more muted when comparing it to the bond market over that same span? The best way to measure that would be to look at the 10 Year Treasury Rate and calculate the compounded returns for holding bonds during this span.

Do the calculation yourself. Go to www.goldisabetterway.com

The compounded total return for the 10 Year Treasury during this span is 238%. A $100,000 investment in bonds in 2000 would be worth roughly $338,700 today. This is still not close to the performance of gold during the same span.

Since most long term investors own both stocks and bonds, the strategy recommended by Wall Street financial institutions, the *average* investor's total return holding both stocks and bonds over the last 18 years is roughly 225%. Gold has simply performed better. What makes this all the more compelling is that the stock and bond markets are on a record nine-year bull run while gold is down!

If these numbers come as a surprise, you are not alone. Of the thousands of investors I've spoken to, the vast majority are shocked when they learn this. Many get angry that no one has shared this information with them. Unfortunately these numbers are about to get worse, not better. The reason? We can no longer expect interest rates to continue lower. From here, we can expect the opposite.

9 THAT WAS THEN, THIS IS NOW

"Money is better than poverty, if only for financial reasons"

Woody Allen

Money Takes A Nap

We all could benefit from a new investment strategy. I believe the risk parity approach of primarily owning stocks and bonds requires re-evaluation. Owning stocks and bonds made a lot of sense at one time. I don't believe this strategy will continue to work. The reason? Investments no longer offer meaningful compounding opportunities.

The definition of investing is *to expend money with the expectation of achieving a profit or material result by putting it into financial schemes, shares or property.* The goal of investing is to achieve a profit. Investing is forward looking. It's about future expectations. What can be lost when considering the goal of our investments is that we may not achieve or realize a *profit* or loss until we sell.

Investing becomes further complicated since our investments can also *produce income*. This is an area where many investors can make big miscalculations. It is this "income generation" portion of investing where I believe Wall Street has been able to propagate a misleading story. These following ideas and strategies about money and investing have been pounded into our brains:

1. **Money never sleeps**
2. **Put your money to work for you**
3. **Stay invested**

Albert Einstein marveled that the greatest invention of all time was *compound interest.* Einstein understood how a lot of things worked, but he was most in awe of the idea of compounding. It's amazing what money can do simply by sitting and compounding. Tremendous wealth has been accumulated over time using this principle. Compounding allows your money to work for you while you sit back and do nothing. Einstein was right! Compounding is an incredible invention.

Rule Of 72

Compounding is the process when an asset's earnings from capital gains or interest, are reinvested to generate additional income over time. The Rule of 72 is a simple and easy compound interest rate formula that tells us how many years it will take money to double including compounded interest. It works the following way. Take the number 72, divide it by the annual interest rates and this will tell you how many years it will take for your money to double by compounding.

If you started with an investment of $100 at an interest rate of 7%, it would take 10.2 years (72/7) for your money to double through compounding. Alternatively, if we know it took 18 years for money to double, we would get to an average compounded interest rate of 4% (72/18).

Image 27
Years to Double Your Money at 7% Interest Rate

The compounded return is calculated each and every year. After the first year you have $107. After two years, $114.49, and so on thereafter. After 10 years we can see that the money doubles to $200. No efforts other than depositing the dollars and letting them do the work for you are necessary. **This basic concept of compounding is essential to understanding the structural challenges the global economy faces today.**

When interest rates are higher, money can more easily *generate income* via compounding. The *historical average* of the 10 Year U.S. Treasury Note is roughly 6%. At 6% interest rates it will take 12 years for money to double. When interest rates are higher, money compounds faster. When interest rates are lower, it takes longer for money to compound.

In a 20 year span from 1980 to 2000, the 10 Year Treasury Rate *averaged* 8.62%. If you invested at this interest rate and let the money compound it would take 8.3 years to double your money. Remember the old maxim? *Put your money in the market and double it every 7 years.* This worked when the 10 Year Treasury offered a robust 8.5% yield. When long-term treasuries offer a meager 3% it's a different story altogether.

Notice that from 1980 to 2000 the stock market went up more

than 12 times. This was a fantastic time to have your money in the equity markets and a terrible time to have invested in gold.

Do the calculation yourself. Go to www.goldisabetterway.com

Notice from 1980 to 2000 the average yield on the 10 Year Treasury was 8.62%. The bond would process excellent returns during this span. When interest rates are at these historically normalized levels owning a selection of *stocks and bonds* makes far more sense than holding gold.

Do the calculation yourself. Go to www.goldisabetterway.com

Perhaps you've been paying attention and realize that interest rates are at historically low levels. They have been manipulated downward by the Federal Reserve and other Central Banks around the world. Over the past 18 years the 10 Year Treasury Rate has *averaged* 3.52%.

Currently the 10 Year Treasury Rate is at 2.4%. If you were to invest in a 10 Year Treasury Note at 2.4% interest rates it would take 30 years for your money to double through compounding.

Over the past two years The Fed has raised rates five times. In a rising rate environment holding bonds can be a poor strategy. Notice that gold's current bull market began in 2016 as The Fed began raising rates. As interest rates continue higher over time, expect the price of gold to rise and perform far better than bonds, which lose value in a rising interest rate environment.

Image 30

10YR TREASURY					GOLD			
START	END	VALUE	AVG YIELD		START	END	CHANGE	%CHANGE
2.24	2.40	$93,333.33	2.08%		$1,060.00	$1,291.00	$231.00	21.79%

$95,416.15   **$121,792.45**

INVESTMENT	START	01/01/2016
$ 100,000	END	01/01/2018

Do the calculation yourself. Go to www.goldisabetterway.com

This is exactly why changing your strategy from only holding stocks and bonds, the financial assets recommended by Wall Street, into holding tangible real assets like gold and silver will offer a far better chance of over performance if rates continue to rise. In this scenario, gold is perfectly positioned for success.

A big question is where will interest rates go in the next several years. If rates continue higher, gold will likely outperform bonds. If there is a sudden downward move in interest rates it will likely signal that the economy is stalling. In this case, gold will likely outperform equities as investors rush to the safe haven of gold. At these levels it's most likely "heads you win, tails you win," for the price of gold regardless of the direction of interest rates.

Interest Rates - Lower For Longer

Even with rates rising, we can expect that they will still remain well below their historical norms for a very long time. The compounding that can occur with rates so low will be poor. It will take money you hold much longer to double than it has in the past.

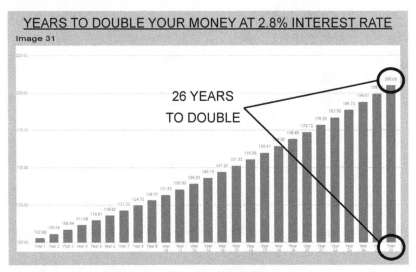

A New Normal Needs A New Strategy

Let's think about interest rates, and dividend yields from stocks and bonds a little differently. Let's compare them to water. If interest rates move significantly higher they are akin to water that goes from room temperature to boiling. Molecules in boiling water move faster. Money when invested will move faster when interest rates are higher, and generate faster growth through compounding. Molecules in cold water move slower. When money is invested and interest rates are low, it will move slower when compounded.

With interest rates at near freezing temperatures, money is barely moving. The strategy that Wall Street wants you to follow is to *stay invested and let your money do the work.* But what happens if money doesn't work, if it's frozen or barely moving? When interest rates are very low, money cannot compound quickly. When that happens it helps to have a different strategy. The *overall value* of the asset must become the main fundamental to focus on and thus where to begin thinking about a new strategy. Valuations become the most important things to consider in a very low interest rate environment.

A popular argument from Wall Street is that equities are not overvalued because interest rates are so low. The CAPE Shiller P/E ratio is currently at 33 times earnings. Wall Street will argue that while that price may *appear* high it's really not because interest rates are so low and money has been forced to flow into equities to find returns. It's an easy argument to understand.

What's also easy to understand is that dividend yields have sunk to all-time lows in the face of this extremely low interest rate environment and *valuations* for stocks and bonds have never been more extreme! What the Wall Street argument omits is the *risk* associated with owning assets at extreme valuations. The only way for this to continue to work for investors is for valuation to continue to go higher and higher indefinitely.

FANG

The technology sector has led the charge in the equity markets and account for a major portion of the boom in the index. The most widely owned stocks today are Facebook, Amazon, Netflix and Google. The FANG stocks all have one thing in common; none of them pay a dividend. There is exclusively only one reason to own these stocks: to sell them to someone else for a higher share price in the future.

Company	P/E Ratio	Dividend
Facebook	36	N/A
Amazon	355	N/A
Netflix	218	N/A
Google	40	N/A

For the FANG stocks, asset value becomes the *only* consideration that matters. One of the biggest knocks against gold by Wall Street is that gold just sits there and doesn't pay a dividend. That's true. It's exactly like owning Facebook, Amazon, Netflix or Google stocks. In fact, there are very few financial assets one can invest in today that are paying a meaningful dividend or yield. Even investments in riskier assets, such as junk bonds, offer historically low yield and find money compounding at a glacial pace. This makes asset value and price the most important consideration to evaluate.

Let's think this through to the logical conclusion. *If asset valuation is really the only metric to consider when acquiring financial assets, the price you pay will ultimately determine the future success of the investment. If valuations are high and above normal range they pose more risk because you may be forced to sell at a lower price in the future. If asset values are low they create opportunity as you have a greater chance of selling them for a higher price in the future.* Stocks and bonds have never been higher. Gold, silver, and other commodities are down an average of 40%. It looks like a good time to sell one and buy the other.

What Interest Rates Tell Us

Low interest rates typically signal weak economies. High interest rates signal inflationary pressures and economies that are running too hot. The goal, and what is *normal*, is to be right down the middle. Not too hot, not too cold.

Interest rates have been on the floor for eight years and have never been this low for this long. With interest rates at historically low levels, it's a signal that the world's economy has been in pretty bad shape for a quite a long time. These low rates are what have caused the massive explosion in all financial assets. Money has flowed into alternative and riskier assets in a hunt for yield and returns. These underlying fundamentals are a main reason why so many financial experts and billionaires are suggesting that long term performance of *all paper assets* over the next ten years is certain to under perform the last ten, and why many are even predicting long term returns will be negative.

Jeremy Grantham suggested exactly that in 2017. Grantham is the Chief Investment strategist at GMO, one of the largest asset managers of funds in the world. His firm has more than $130 Billion under management. Grantham is regarded as among the world's most knowledgeable investors and has been particularly noted for his ability to spot bubbles. He has been a vocal critic of the various governmental responses to the Global Financial Crisis. Grantham's prediction for the next seven years is actually negative for *both* stocks and bonds.

If you are wondering how can this be, look no further than long term interest rates. Many experts believe that long term rates are going to remain very low for a very long time. Taking the rule of 72, and projecting a 10 Year Treasury at 4%, we are likely looking at another 18 years for assets to double from these levels. *Actual* expert predictions have the long term interest rate even lower at just 3%. At 3% you can expect to wait 24 years for your assets to double.

Perhaps *money never sleeps*, but it no longer *works* either. Investing with a strategy that assumes it still does is like trying to drink a cup of frozen water - it's not very effective. Which is why it's time for a new strategy.

It's time to own assets that are undervalued, like commodities and precious metals. The big knock on commodities is that they do not pay a dividend. Well, neither does almost anything else these days. As discussed earlier, the FANG stocks that most people own offer no dividend. With equities up over 300% from their floor in 2009, and with most commodities down roughly 40% in the same time, doesn't it make logical sense to be selling overvalued equities while they are still high and buying undervalued commodities and precious metals while they are still low?

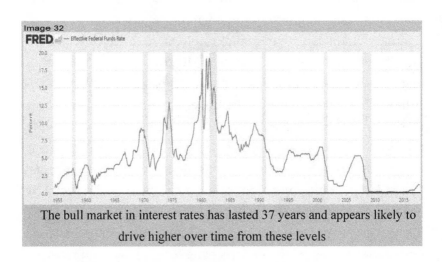

The bull market in interest rates has lasted 37 years and appears likely to drive higher over time from these levels

10

RISK

I'm All In!

The idea of putting *money to work* is the foundation for the popular modern investing strategies that suggest investors should be "all in, all the time". We have been programmed to believe that the right way to invest is to put our money in the markets and *let it work* for us. Wall Street tells us the best way to drive returns is to "stay invested".

As a general rule, investment dollars will flow where they can get their greatest return. Oftentimes when markets collapse the best investment dollars are those that lose the least. Having your money *uninvested* and in cash or in a safe haven such as gold is a much better strategy when markets implode. When the dotcoms imploded in 2000, equity markets dropped over 40%. When the housing bubble popped many investors lost more than 50%. Investors with an all-in strategy suffered dramatic losses in the aftermath of the last two financial crises. Investors holding cash didn't lose. Investors holding gold saw 2.5X gains in the years following each crisis.

Wall Street will never support moving your money into cash or tangible physical assets like gold. If they did they would be unable to earn the fees that are their lifeblood. Believe it or not, registered investment advisors and financial professionals can lose their jobs for *selling away.* Selling away in the US brokerage industry is deemed inappropriate for a registered representative, stockbroker, or financial advisor who sells their clients or solicits the sale of assets and securities not held or offered by the brokerage firm they represent. The financial services industry have made it very difficult for financial professionals to offer *any* alternative advice. Professionals that do can even lose their jobs.

The boom and bust markets that have been created by the Federal Reserve bubble machine over the past 30 years have spooked a lot retail investors. Many are worried that the last decade's boom in the stock market may be the biggest bubble ever created. There is a famous saying that goes 'Fool me once shame on you, fool me twice shame on me.'

At the same time human nature is incredibly powerful and this adds to the challenge. The folks that have played it safe while financial markets have inflated can see themselves as *patsies* because they are missing out while most others are making money. FOMO, *(fear of missing out),* is one of the strongest magnets pulling investors into taking treacherous risks. Unfortunately, for most people, the pull becomes the strongest when the risks are the greatest and assets are most overvalued. This is exactly where we stand today. Risks have never been greater.

Managing Risk

Wall Street doesn't want us to think about money being "at risk." *Investing* sounds different than *gambling.* Gambling insinuates winning or losing, whereas investing insinuates growth and returns. The reality is that all investments carry risk. Stocks, bonds, mutual funds, ETF's, real estate, gold and silver can all lose value, perhaps even all of their value, if market conditions turn sour. Even *conservative* investments such as certificates of deposit issued by a bank or cash issued by the Federal Reserve come with inflation and default risk. Physical metals have one innate advantage: no risk of total impairment

Wall Street's solution, and the way they keep most investors fully invested, is to suggest a *diversification* among the assets held in a portfolio. This *diversified* approach is meant to offer a hedge to investors by recommending the holding of non-correlated assets that will perform differently given certain varying circumstances. The idea with this diversification strategy is that while some assets in a portfolio may lose value at certain times, others in the portfolio will gain at the exact same time and offset those losses.

For Wall Street that diversified strategy has been a recommendation for investors to practice *risk parity* and hold *stocks and bonds*. Wall Street has gone to great lengths to instill this strategy in investors minds as the *correct* way to invest. In fact just say "stocks and....?" and virtually every person will say bonds. It's like salt *and* pepper, shampoo *and* conditioner, peanut butter *and* jelly. Stocks *and* bonds. That's just what we all have been programmed to know.

You may be familiar with investment models that recommend that we should hold more stocks when we are younger. Then as we get older our portfolios should rotate into holding more bonds. The idea behind this strategy has been that stocks are riskier and younger investors have more time to overcome losses, whereas bonds are meant to be less risky and therefore more appropriate for older investors who do not have the same risk tolerance or amount of time to recoup losses.

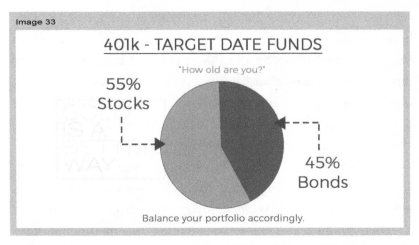

This risk management strategy of owning stocks and bonds based on age has been pounded into our brains by Wall Street. Entire 401k investment plans now have names that try and lead investors down a particular path including even naming the funds *Target Date Funds* and allowing investors to project future earnings by plugging in a future date.

What gets completely lost on the average investor looking at these target date funds offered in so many retirement plans is that the future account balance projections may be entirely misleading.

The fine print of every financial disclosure offered in by any investment advisor will tell us *past investment performance is not indicative of future results.* Yet these plans then use the *last 50 years of averages* to prompt unsuspecting employees to select them in the expectation that the future will be the same as the past, which it most assuredly will not. Their formulas use returns earned in the 1980's and 1990's when calculating their overall averages. This skews their numbers higher and underestimates the lower return environment we have been in for an extended period of time and will remain in for the foreseeable future.

The Everything Bubble

What happens when both stocks and bonds are inflated at the same time? What happens when low interest rates are the *cause* of not only inflated stock values, but also the *cause* of the inflated values of bonds? Most investors are holding bonds in their portfolio as a hedge. How can bonds be a hedge to the most expensive stocks market in history when bonds themselves have never been more expensive and lower yields?

Target date funds that are calculated using averages that are skewed over longer periods of time may be misleading the consumer by overestimating future gains. One of the greatest points of emphasis in this entire book is that stocks and bonds are more correlated today than they have ever been. Perhaps the greatest value I can provide is helping you examine if the diversification strategy of owning stocks and bonds offers the same protection that it once did when interest rates were more normalized.

The most obvious and major risk to Wall Street's *all-in* diversification strategy of holding stocks and bonds, is the tremendous loss that will be incurred should interest rates surge higher from existing levels. This event could cause both bonds and stocks to lose value at the same time.

This interest rate risk currently seems to be completely under-anticipated by Wall Street, especially in lieu of The Fed entering into a tightening cycle. Rates are rising and are projected to continue doing so over the next several years.

If I could shout from the mountain tops with a global megaphone, these are the main questions I would scream to the world: **How can you be protected or diversified when everything you own has been inflated due to near freezing interest rates? How can holding inflated assets that are now completely correlated be considered diversified? What happens if interest rates surge?**

The obvious answer is that employing Wall Street's risk parity strategy when interest rates fly higher may be the *most* risky strategy not the *least*. If you want to avoid risk and have a truly diversified portfolio today, you must look to own asset classes that are *not correlated* with one another.

Can You Afford To Gamble With Your Financial Future?

I met the famous comedian Louie Anderson (Family Feud) when I was producing my first film back in my entertainment days. I had cast Louie in my film *Do It For Uncle Manny* and was honored that a comedian of his caliber would even entertain the idea of being in my movie, much less agreeing to do it. It sparked a real friendship and he invited me, along with my producing partner, to come to Las Vegas one weekend and watch him perform. We went to see Louie perform in front of 3,000 people and it was among the best stand-up shows I have ever seen. Afterwards Louie gave us me an insider's look at Las Vegas. He walked us around the casino and pointed out in his hilarious way why Vegas will always win.

His conclusion was not because the odds were in favor of the house, which of course make it impossible to win over time. Louie pointed out that the real reason the house will always win is that, *psychologically,* every gambler has a *limit* to what they can *lose* and *no limit* to what they can *win*. This mentality is what keeps almost every non-professional from being able to leave Vegas a winner. Louie told me about a guy that came to Vegas with $500 and then turned it into $50,000 after hitting an incredible hot streak at the blackjack table. He then commented he's seen it happen dozens of times but they almost always go home broke.

The reason? These gamblers had no limit to what they could win. Rather than walk away and lock up profits, gamblers have a tendency to *let it ride* and keep pushing until the odds inevitably wipe them out.

He later introduced me to his friend who Louie called the 'best gambler I have ever seen.' Louie's friend was a professional gambler who managed to have a great deal of success and was able to make a living playing blackjack. I was so fascinated and I needed to know what his *secret* was. Was he able to count cards? Did he have a system? If so, I wanted to know what it was.

I'll never forget what Louie's friend told me; "Successful gambling is not about a system, it's all about *money management.* Clearly the odds are in the favor of the casino and I know that. However, I can win more than I lose because I know how to manage my money. I have limits to what I can lose and, more importantly, *I have limits on what I can win.* Once I hit those limits I walk away, no matter what, and it's that discipline that allows me to do this for a living, because not only am I willing to sit down and play, I am also willing to walk away."

That advice may be more relevant and more important for investors now than anytime in history. With interest rates at these historically low levels. With both stocks and bonds on a near decade long bull run (second longest in history) having produced over 300% gains since bottoming out in 2009. With stocks and bonds also more correlated than at anytime in history. You must recognize that what has before been called investing, today may really not be much different than gambling. The question is, are you willing to take your profit and walk away?

I believe that *buy and hold* is no longer the most effective strategy. How can it be when money is asleep and virtually no income can be earned holding these assets? In a boom and bust environment fueled by debt, where markets can collapse, we need a *buy and sell* strategy. Buy assets that are undervalued and sell before they deflate or collapse. In today's markets it's better to have limits on both your downside *and* on your upside. You must be cognizant of stretched valuations and understand that these assets can devalue faster than you can even move to exit them.

What Were We Thinking?

The liquidity created by the Federal Reserve and other Central Banks around the globe have created a tremendous amount of cheap money. This cheap money has fueled an inflation in virtually all financial asset prices.

I believe we will look back at 2017, in hindsight, five years from now with a similar thought to what happened after the dot-com boom and the housing boom. That thought will be a sorrowful regret for too many people after this bubble implodes, one where everyone will sing the blues in unison. The name of that tune? *What were we thinking?!*

Amazon, which pays no dividend, trades at 300X earnings? ***What were we thinking?!***

European junk bonds pay a paltry 2.5% yield? ***What were we thinking?!***

Bitcoin goes from $11,000 to $16,000 in one day? ***What were we thinking?!***

$6 Trillion in worldwide sovereign debt pays a negative yield? ***What were we thinking?!***

The U.S. National Debt explodes above $20 Trillion and we pass a spending bill that adds trillions more to the deficit. ***What were we thinking?!***

A 12" x 17" DaVinci that may or may not be authentic sells for $450 Million. ***What were we thinking?!***

GOLDEN NUGGET #4

Things that make you go "Hmmm..."

Buy Gold! A Strategy for Rising Rates

When interest rates rise over time, paper assets struggle. The last time we had an extended rising interest rate period was from 2003 through 2006 when The Fed Funds Rate went from 1% to 5.5%. Bonds were negative during this period. Gold, by contrast, rose 84%, dramatically outperforming paper assets.

The last time the 10 Year Treasury *doubled* was from 1977 to 1980. The Fed *expects* the 10 Year Treasury to double over the next few years. As this occurs expect stocks and bond to struggle mightily while physical gold soars to unseen heights.

103

III HOW WE GOT HERE

11   NOSTALGIA

"I wish there was a way to know you were in the good old
days before you actually left them"

Andy Bernard

The Why Behind Markets

What's the first thing you would do if your car broke down on the side of the road? I know I personally open up the hood and take a look. I'm not a mechanic so while I can do that, I will have no idea if what I'm looking at is broken or not. So for me, looking under the hood is a mostly useless exercise, but it's something to do while I wait for AAA. I believe that many investors have this same feeling when looking at the stock and bond markets and trying to understand where and how to invest. It's like looking at a car engine and having no experience as a mechanic.

Looking at numbers is one thing but *understanding them and the underlying **why*** behind them is something completely different. Let's unpack the story of the last 35 years and *why* markets performed so differently in the 1980's and 1990's than they have since 2000.

Let's take a look at some of the fundamental reasons why the equity markets used to perform so well, and why investors aren't seeing the same results now.

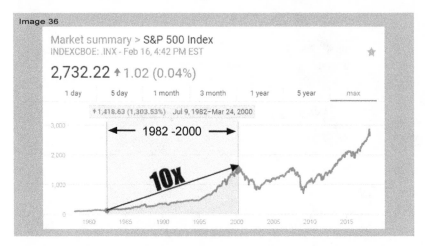

Image 36

Market summary > S&P 500 Index
INDEXCBOE: .INX - Feb 16, 4:42 PM EST

2,732.22 ↑1.02 (0.04%)

1 day   5 day   1 month   3 month   1 year   5 year   max

↑1,418.63 (1,303.53%)   Jul 9, 1982–Mar 24, 2000

1982 -2000

On July 9th, 1982 the S&P 500 traded at 109 points. Roughly 18 years later the S&P is trading at 1,303 points which is a whopping gain of 1,200% in this time span. An annual average gain of a massive 15% per year.

What happened in the early 1980's that really drove this market performance? If you look at Image 36 above, you can see that prior to 1982 the markets were flat. It's not until the early 1980's that they actually start to drive higher on a positive incline. While there are many factors we could discuss, I believe there are two main factors most responsible for this performance that warrant the deepest look:

1. Boom!

More than 10,000 people were born every day between 1946 and 1961. During this time the population of the United States exploded, growing from roughly 125 million people in 1940, to 250 million people just fifty years later. At the time, this marked the greatest population increase in history.

Why is this important? When looking at the equity markets, the most important fundamental is *growth*. When we invest in a company we are investing in their *future growth*. Demographically, the U.S. was booming in the early 1980's. We had an expanding population that provided huge demand for food, energy, housing, automobiles, entertainment and other consumable goods. It is *demand* that fueled the U.S. economy during these two decades. This expanding population was also *producing* more than at any other time in history.

When growth is booming, corporations can be expected to make more revenue and profit due to an underlying demand for the products they produce. Beginning in the early 1980's there were more people who were making more money than ever before. *Boomers* entered their prime earning years during this time. As these baby boomers earned more money, they then bought more cars and homes, spent more money, and became the first *consumption generation*. Business for American corporations was booming!

The 1980's were defined by excess and the new spending habits of this massive pool of people. All of this demand led to larger economic growth and higher prices in asset classes.

Demand built on the foundation of growth leads to healthy inflation. In other words, if demand is growing faster than supply, prices will increase. Demographically, the baby boom generation increased productivity which in turn provided a growth in *demand* and, as the U.S. economy grew, prices went higher.

2. Employer Sponsored Plans

Focusing exclusively on demographics misses one major part of this puzzle. It's important not only to look at *who* created this new demand, but also *where* that demand was directed. In addition to consumer products like cars and homes, boomers also helped Wall Street sell more goods and services in the form of securities, namely stocks and bonds. The baby boomers were the first main generation to invest their earnings into the stock market. The peak earning years for the average individual are between the ages of 38 and 52 years of age. This is the time most people begin investing in earnest. Beginning in the early 1980's, a great deal of *new investment demand* was seen for the very first time in the stock market. Think about a stock like any other product - when demand to purchase is strong, share prices will increase as more buyers than sellers will inflate a stock's share price.

The first 401k plan was created in 1978. A 401k is a retirement plan offered by employers that allow workers to contribute a portion of weekly salaries into a personal retirement account. By the early 1980's the 401k, and other employer sponsored plans (401, 403A, 403B, TSP), had become the norm for employees.

Prior to this time, if you were an employee you likely had a *pension*. A pension is a plan where the employer promises a *defined benefit* after retirement, typically a percentage of one's salary vested by length of employment. Prior to the 1980's employees didn't get to *choose* where their money was invested because corporations handled that for them.

During the early 1980's corporations were able to transfer this responsibility of maintaining pension plans off their books, and were able to shift this responsibility into the hands of their employees. For the first time in history employees were now making regular contributions to their retirement accounts. These contributions were often incentivized with matching contributions made by the employer.

Anyone with one of these employer sponsored plans knows that the *choices* for allocation are usually a handful of *mutual funds*, virtually all of which are tied to the stock market. Beginning in full force in the early 1980's there was a powerful one-two punch that caused massive growth in the stock and bond markets over the next 15 years coming from boomers and their 401k's.

Mutual funds were sold to investors as better way to invest. These securities allowed investors to participate in the growth and performance of certain sectors and indexes without having to take on the risk of holding individual stocks. The idea was that, by spreading the risk across multiple stocks, investors would be more protected should any one company go belly up. These funds were in turn managed by investment professionals. Retail investors wouldn't need to become experts on stock picking.

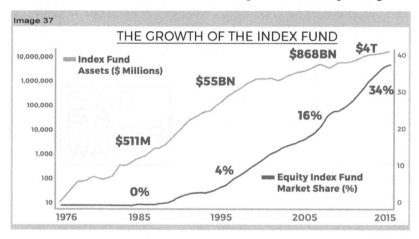

The chart above highlights the dramatic increase in capital inflows into index funds in the last 30 years. Notice that in 1985 the amount of cash invested in index funds was a mere $500 Million. Just 10 years later that amount would be 100 times higher at a total of $55 Billion. Another 20 years after that it is nearly 100 times higher at over $4 Trillion.

The massive boom and growth of the stock market was significantly impacted by the choices these employees, turned new investors, were given. Owning real estate or precious metals and other alternatives were not among the *choices* that employees with these plans have ever been offered. Employees have only ever been offered a selection of mutual funds tied to the stock market.

The net result? More people, (baby boomers specifically), making more money than ever before and putting a part of their paycheck into their 401k and other similar plans every single week. All of which are then tied to the stock market in the form of mutual funds. All of this buying would lead to higher and higher share prices.

Not a bad recipe for success. It is easy to see why from the early 1980s to 2000 you have this self replicating loop where the markets went higher and higher and higher. This 18 year period (1982 to 2000) is the greatest growth period in our stock market's history. The onslaught of new people in the form of baby boomers investing in the markets for the first time was a primary driver of this economic activity.

The demographic explosion of the baby boomers and the phasing out of pensions in favor of employee plans were the main catalysts for tremendous stock market and bond market returns from 1982 to 2000.

12 SMOKE AND MIRRORS

*"The great enemy of truth is very often not the lie,
deliberate, contrived and dishonest, but the myth;
persistent, persuasive and unrealistic"*

John F. Kennedy

You Sure This Is Good for Me?

When comparing the 1980's and 1990's to the last 18 years, the first thing we can notice is a dramatically different line structure in the stock market trend line. No longer is the trend line in the stock market on a nice steady incline higher. Since the late 1990's our markets would better be described as boom and bust, boom and bust, boom and..? Well, maybe a bust comes next. We don't know.

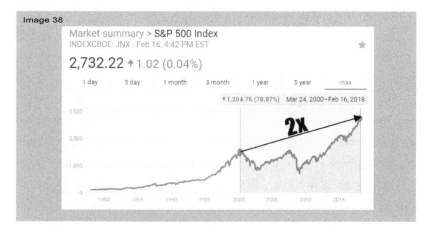

Image 38

The S&P 500 traded at 1,524 points on March 24th, 2000. 18 years later, on January 2nd, 2018 it would trade at 2,695 points. This equals an increase of a paltry 76% during this time. An average annual increase of 5.5% per year.

But why? Why did markets perform so differently before versus now? Understanding the *why* behind how markets have performed over the last 18 years will provide essential evidence that we may be able use to infer a better understanding of what's likely to come next.

Demand Fueled By Debt

If the 1980s and 1990s were fueled by demand from *growth*, the 2000s and the 2010's have been fueled by demand from *debt*.

Any discussion on the performance of the stock market over time must include a serious mention of The Federal Reserve. The Federal Reserve is our country's Central Bank. It is also effectively the Central Bank of the world, since the dollar is the world's trading currency. For our purposes it's important to understand the mandate of The Fed and the tools that our Central Bank uses to meet its directive. And how, by trying to achieve that mandate, they have become a *player* that can have tremendous impact on the paper markets.

The mandate of The Fed is to create maximum employment (unemployment of 5%), stable prices (2% inflation), and to moderate long-term interest rates. The tools by which The Fed accomplishes this directive are by controlling the money supply and interest rates (Fed Funds Rate.) When The Fed wants to *stimulate* the economy, it will increase the money supply and *lower interest rates*. This is known as *loosening*. When The Fed wants to *slow down* the economy that is overheating, they will *raise interest rates* and diminish the money supply. This is called *tightening*. When the Fed is *loose*, equity markets have historically *inflated*. When the Fed *tightens,* markets often lose value or *drop*.

Remember the Ham and Cheese Sandwich experiment - when money supply was increased, prices rose. When the money supply was decreased, prices fell.

The Maestro

Alan Greenspan was the Federal Reserve Chairman from 1987 through 2007 and served a historic five terms under four separate presidents. He was initially chosen by Ronald Reagan and he would go on to serve under George Bush, Bill Clinton, and George Bush Jr.

Greenspan was often referred to as 'The Maestro.' He was the conductor and the markets were his orchestra. The music they played made investors rich. When Greenspan spoke he would use intentionally confusing language, (dubbed "Greenspeak" by many financial analysts), that made it difficult to predict what exactly he would do next with monetary policy. This *obfuscation,* coupled with the significant overall positive performance of the equity markets while under his watch, earned him The Maestro moniker. His policies are widely regarded as responsible for the great market performance during this period of time. There are also many today that blame Greenspan for the current Everything Bubble.

Alan Greenspan's first day in office actually took place two months prior to Black Monday in 1987, when the stock market dropped 22% in one day. This epic one day decline is what Alan Greenspan was welcomed to as the new Fed Chairman after only a few weeks on the job. What Greenspan would do in this moment would become his signature move anytime crises rose that spooked the marketplace. In 1987, the action Greenspan took was to immediately drop the Fed Funds rate in an effort to create liquidity in the market.

It began what would become his consistent move - to stave off dramatic declines in the equity markets, he would manipulate interest rates. That action would ultimately drive markets higher. As you can see in Image 39 below, when Greenspan lowered interest rates in 1987 to create liquidity, the market recovered very quickly.

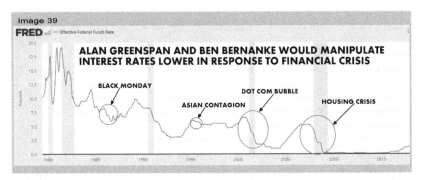

1997 brought with it the next crisis. This one was a currency crisis deemed the *Asian Contagion* that came along coupled with the *Russian Ruble Crisis.* Emerging market currency crises around the world caused equity markets to drop dramatically around the globe. Greenspan hopped into action and lowered the Fed Funds Rate from 6% to 4% and markets quickly regained their footing.

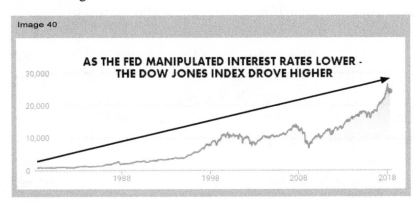

The lower interest rates in 1997 were soon followed by an equity market explosion. Markets would go up a whopping 56% in the next 21 months as dot com mania, coupled with cheap money, created the highest overvaluation in stock market history.

If Easy Credit Leads To Asset Bubbles, It Is The *Tightening* Of That Credit That Causes Bubbles To Pop

As dotcom's exploded higher in the late 1990's, Greenspan raised interest rates. By 2000, with P/E ratios at over 40 times earnings and Greenspan tightening Monetary policy, the perfect bubble then perfectly popped.

Rising interest rates ended the dot com party. The S&P 500 would quickly go on to lose roughly 47% in a span of about 30 months. The NASDAQ would lose over 80% of its value as dotcoms imploded.

What did Alan Greenspan do in response? Once again, he came to the rescue by dramatically lowering the Fed Funds Rate, this time to 1%. Within months the markets started moving higher. This action positioned interest rates at the lowest levels since The Great Depression. This ultra low rate environment gave birth to the *housing boom*.

Anyone who remembers the housing boom remembers one thing: money was not only cheap, it was also very accessible. Remember, inflation is defined as too much money chasing too few goods. The housing bubble is the perfect example of how this transpires. The money in this case was initially provided by mortgage lenders offering incredibly low interest rate loans to home buyers. Mortgage loans were easy to come by and almost anyone who desired was given access to money to buy a home. All of this *demand, fueled by debt,* caused home prices to soar higher as there was far too much money chasing too little inventory.

With Greenspan, the way investors perceived market risk would

117

change. Greenspan's moves allowed investors to take more risks with the knowledge that The Fed always had their back should markets fall. Many economists argue that The Fed, by inserting itself so directly with interest rate manipulation, would create the boom and bust traits that markets have seemed to inherit since. Lowering interest rates helped fuel the bubbles and raising of rates then pops these bubbles. It's a cycle that has required more aggressive and looser policies from The Fed each time it repeats.

Easy credit leads to asset bubbles. It was the easy credit created in the late 1997 that really fueled the dot com boom. It was the easy credit created by Alan Greenspan that created the housing boom. It's the easiest credit in history that has led to the Everything Bubble.

Ultimately when interest rates rise into these overvalued asset bubbles, the result is collapsing of bubbles. The financial collapse that was caused when rates went higher in the peak of the housing bubble was so massive that when it popped it almost brought down the entire global economy.

Rather than feel the pain and rebuild after the collapse, The Fed again jumped into action. Ben Bernanke was now leading the way as Chairman of The Fed. Bernanke would take a play from Alan Greenspan's book, pushed it to the extreme, and lowered interest rates to 0%. A rate this low had not been contemplated since the Great Depression. When that didn't work to stem the disaster, he did something even more aggressive than Greenspan had ever done. He printed roughly $4.5 Trillion. Hence his moniker 'Helicopter Ben' dropping bags of money from the sky.

Forcing Demand Through Debt - Quantitative Easing

One important question begs to be discussed: when $4.5 Trillion of new money is created out of thin air, where does all that money go? It's an important question. Let's first address where this money did not go. It didn't go to the little guy who needed to make his rent or car payment and was really struggling. Bankers weren't lending to those types of individuals anymore. If you wanted a loan in the years after the housing collapse, you better not have needed it. Only those that didn't need the money were granted access. Banks and wealthy individuals were the beneficiaries of the free money created out of thin air. As a result almost all of this new money went to one place: Wall Street.

Let's Not Invest, Let's Eat - Stock Buybacks

It's what Wall Street did with this borrowed money that has inflated the stock market to where it is today. Equity values have inflated more than 300%, not because of revenue growth and real demand, but in large part due to Wall Street's aggressive stock buy backs. Wall Street corporations have bought back their stock with borrowed new money created out of thin air by Central Banks. The *costs?* Virtually *free* since interest rates have been on the floor.

Beginning in 2008, Central Banks around the globe have followed the same program of QE, printing over $6 Trillion in new money. This is represented in Image 41. Notice that Central Banks have taken massive debt onto their balance sheets. All of this new money has fueled the biggest financial bubble in human history. Do you notice the rise in the S&P 500 correlates exactly with the rise in debt?

This *debt cocktail* will kill us as interest rates surge higher. Just like it did in 2000 and 2008. Only this time when the black swan of default comes flying in there may be no way to stave it off. This time investors will not only lose, they may lose everything.

Images 41 and 42, when viewed together, are alarming! If you believe equity markets are at the highest valuations in history due to strong economies, you have drank the proverbial *kool aid*.

119

You're not alone. *Everyone has drank the kool aid. I believe it's a liquid that is poison.*

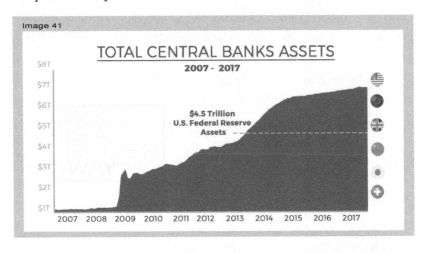

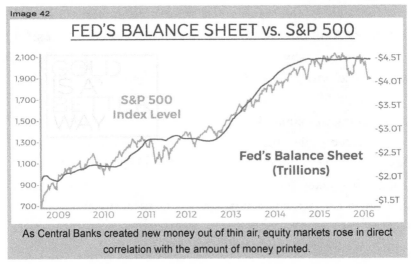

As Central Banks created new money out of thin air, equity markets rose in direct correlation with the amount of money printed.

Warren Buffet has a saying of which I am reminded when I look at the surveys of investors who are more bullish today than at any time in history. Buffet says: "Our markets have 10 year cycles, it's a shame we only have seven year memories."

High investor confidence is often an indicator of overvalued markets. When confidence is this high it's often followed by large pullbacks and corrections.

Central Bank's fat finger buying is one of the main reasons for equities being at all time highs. This has allowed for never before seen leverage. As investors lever up, asset values inflate. It's the coming de-leveraging that you must prepare for. When it comes it will bring massive pain to all those unprepared. Getting caught up in the euphoria and bullish momentum of today's markets may work in the short term. But if you are not getting out now, when will you?

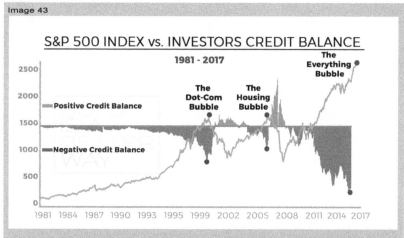

Image 43

Investor confidence, coupled with low interest rates allows for leverage. Investments in the market are often made with borrowed money. As investors borrow to invest, equity markets drive higher.

It seems logical that we are at all time highs in the paper markets because of inflated balance sheets of Central Banks and tremendous leverage in the system due to low rates. When leverage diminishes, rates rise, and Central Banks begin to reduce their balance sheets, it will have a negative impact on equities. One of the best indicators that markets are due for correction is when they are overbought. They are the most overbought in history! It is simply a matter of time before this reverses in a big way.

Which all begs some very important questions; What happens when Central Banks stop acquiring assets and actually begin reducing their balance sheets? What happens when interest rates surge higher and de-leveraging occurs? Who will buy when markets collapse?

13

DEBT

"Neither a Borrower nor a Lender Be"

Polonius - Hamlet, Act I

It Never Ends Well

When I was in college I learned a fantastic lesson about debt. It's a lesson that college kids since the late 1980's have experienced first hand, and it's a great example from which to begin a discussion about debt.

I started at Temple University in 1987. One of my very first memories was freshman initiation. It's the time when universities officially introduce the incoming class of freshmen to the school. I remember walking around wide eyed at the sheer size and scope of the school. During orientation you register for classes, spend time with other students and learn your way around campus. Excitement levels are very high. Everything is new. Not only do incoming students first learn the history and traditions of the school, they are also introduced to credit!

Lined up along the entire campus during orientation week were credit card companies offering students credit cards. I remember seeing massive displays for Visa, Discover and American Express all promoting their cards.

Signing up was so easy. Simply fill out a form and you were

guaranteed to receive a credit card. My very first card was a Discover Card with a $300 limit. This was the best thing ever. They were actually giving me free money to go and spend. It was awesome... for a while.

As an incoming college student I didn't have a job. My *job* was to go to school and study. Any free time I had from class was meant to be spent preparing and learning. That study was meant to be an investment in my future. I could have used my new credit card to further invest in my future. I could have used it to buy books, a computer, or tutors and other items that would have enhanced my ability to do my job better and allow me to be a more productive student.

As a college freshman, in reality, the main and most important expenditures to me were pizza and beer. Now armed with my trusty new Discover Card I could get anything I wanted. Oh boy, did I take advantage of the new free money I had gained. Not only did I have new money for food, beer, clothes and other things that are so valuable to a college freshman, I also turned all of my friends onto the same scheme. If any one of our cards had a limit that had been hit, another one was there to pick up the tab.

After I ran up the card to the limit I quickly learned that I had something called a *minimum payment due*. That first minimum payment was $32 and I remember thinking, *where am I going to get the money to pay for that?* My problem was that my card was no longer good for purchases as I had used up all of the available credit. Now it was a burden that I was suddenly responsible for.

My friend George had a great idea. He said, "Why don't you do what I did, and just go get another credit card, and use that to pay off your Discover Card?" I hadn't thought of that!

And so that is exactly what I did. I went and got a Masterard, and the deal got even better. This time, because I had made a few on-time payments on my Discover Card, I now was being offered a limit of $1,000 on my new credit card. This was $700 more than the $300 limit I was offered by Discover. This credit thing was just too good to be true! From there, rather than tighten my spending habits and pay down my debt, I did the opposite. Armed with more free money I used my new card to make the minimum payment on my Discover Card. I then proceeded to burn through the Masterard. Next up was Visa, because it was '*Everywhere I wanted to be.*'

I learned another important lesson about credit during this time. My credit rating would go down due to excessive borrowing. The new cards also carried a much higher interest rate than the first ones I had. I was now a bigger credit risk. While companies were still willing to lend to me for a short time, it was going to cost me a whole lot more for the same amount of access due to my higher rates. I learned first hand how rising interest rates cost me even more money on debt I had *already* incurred.

And for a while I was able to spend even more money that I didn't have. Before long that plan all caught up with me. I had maxed out my credit limit on all of my credit cards. In the end I was faced with a few thousand dollars in credit card debt. Then the pain began.

Instead of studying and focusing on my education, I was forced to get a real job. Ironically the job I ended up with was as a pizza delivery guy for the campus pizza shop. While other kids were having fun partying on Friday and Saturday nights, I was now the guy delivering their pizza. How quickly debt had taken me from joy to pain.

To make matters worse for those that love me, my grandfather, mother and older brother most specifically, were unwittingly forced to become my new lenders once banks stopped lending to me in order to help me make ends meet. That's the nice thing about my family. While my credit rating may have been 521 with the credit rating agencies, my family was there to pick me up and lend to me despite knowing the likelihood of seeing a return payment was extremely low. I was lucky that they had the money to help me.

The amount of stress and embarrassment caused by taking on debt obligations that I was unable to afford consumed much of my time and energy. Instead of enjoying my college career to the fullest like some of my friends that weren't in the same situation, my life was a series of borrowing from Peter to pay Paul. This constant juggling, and my ongoing austerity thereafter, was a very painful experience.

Despite eventually paying the credit card companies far more than I initially spent, I would later default on some of these credit card obligations. My debt burden was ultimately so great that even while I made payments for several years throughout school, (and even in the few years thereafter), I could never get out from under the debt pile. Ultimately I defaulted, my credit rating was ruined, and it would take me seven years before I would even be considered creditworthy again. In order to become credit worthy again I needed to live within my means and *earn* more than I *spent*. This time around I needed to rebuild my credit slowly over time. It was not until many years later that I was able to repay all of the debts to my family that I had incurred.

This experience taught me an invaluable lesson about credit and debt. I learned first hand how by using credit, I was able to pull forward my *future earnings* to enjoy what I wanted in the present. I also learned that all of that debt had a future cost. I would need to earn more later on to pay it all off and far more than I initially spent.

My story, as it turns out, has a lot of similarities to the debt crisis the world now finds itself in. Each step of my personal debt crisis has similarities that we can identify in evaluating where we are today.

Phase One: Debt Appears The Same As Demand

When I first began running up my credit card on purchases of pizza and beer, it had the effect of looking like *real* demand. The campus pizza place was selling me more pizza and Budweiser was selling me more beer. All of my new demand, allowed for by my new credit facility, appeared as real demand to these businesses that were able to generate revenue from my debt. My personal debt was someone else's revenue. The reality was my demand was actually created because I had *credit available* to me. Of course I wanted to consume pizza and beer but these were desires that I would have forsaken had I not had available credit. Or better still, desires I would have necessarily only filled through my own production and earnings had I not had credit available to me.

Phase Two: Debt Is Allowed to Grow As Interest Rates Are Lowered

The *good credit* I established by paying my earliest bills on time and servicing the interest due allowed me to take on further credit. As I took on more debt and established a payment history I was considered more creditworthy. It allowed me to borrow more. This additional credit facility further allowed me to continue my personal spending habits. My demand fueled by debt only further supported the revenue streams of the campus pizza place and the local beer distributor.

Phase Three: Credit Tightens Forcing Higher Debt Service And Decreased Spending

As I took on more and more debt and began slow-paying my obligations, credit card companies were no longer eager to lend at lower rates. I could still take on additional debt, but now

127

it was offered at a higher premium and required higher debt service if I wanted to continue my ongoing demand. Now, the payments on my credit cards were putting great pressure on me, ultimately forcing me to get a job and earn income in order to stay afloat.

Phase Four: Tightening Credit Caused A Change In My Demand And Consumption

With credit drying up I was forced to change my consumption habits. I could no longer afford pizza and beer. If I wanted to consume these college staples I needed to produce and earn. At this point in the cycle I needed to earn far more than what I wanted to consume as my debt service obligations continued higher. Interest rates on my personal debt were going higher and higher. *This forced me to earn more and spend less.*

Phase Five: Debt Burdens Become Too Great Leading to Default

I was unable to continue living at the same standard. Not only was I forced to dramatically reduce my consumption, I eventually was unable to produce and earn enough money to cover even my most basic living needs of food and rent as well as pay the service on my debt. Eventually the only way out of this debt trap was to default.

The Business Cycle

This five step process is very similar to what many experts call the business cycle. The business cycle is a sequence of leveraging and deleveraging that takes place within economies all over the world. It's the natural order of things. It is cyclical. The business cycle is propelled by leveraging and deleveraging of the credit cycle. The business cycle feels like a boom when countries, corporations, and individuals are leveraging up as their consumption grows. As the cycle continues however, and credit tightens, the feeling of the boom stagnates and flattens out. Ultimately the cycle becomes recessionary. As the necessary deleveraging then occurs, demand slows, consumption is restricted and debts get paid down. After the economy deleverages, the cycle begins anew.

The Housing Bubble that popped in 2007 is evidence of what can be caused by tightening of the credit cycle. The Fed was in the process of raising rates and was projected to continue until rates had normalized. Due to the large amount of leverage in the real estate market during this time, home prices had become overvalued and had created a huge bubble. The tightening by The Federal Reserve popped the bubble with such a powerful force that unprecedented extreme measures were now necessary just to keep the world afloat.

Those extreme measures were the opposite of austerity and belt tightening. As explained earlier, the measures called for were lowering interest rates to 0% and then when that wasn't sufficient, included adding over $6 Trillion to the money supply. These actions were meant to be temporary quick fixes. Rather, they were extended for nine years and have allowed for an explosion of debt not just in the U. S. but around the globe.

Many argue that had The Fed not stepped in we could still be in a deep recession. I recently heard it claimed that The Fed was brave to make the decisions they made. Really? Would it not have been far more brave to let the free market systems and capitalism work instead of bailing out the banks and the elites on Wall Street? What people may miss in this whole equation is that The Federal Reserve itself is a bank and what they did would better be defined as self preservation rather than brave.

We will never know where we would have been otherwise

because The Fed did step in. In doing so they became the backstop for Wall Street. They have encouraged more risk and bad behavior as investors can now assume that The Fed will bail them out again when the next crisis occurs.

The Fed created $4.5 Trillion of new money through their asset purchase and bond buying programs. They were not alone. The Central Banks of Europe, Japan, Switzerland, Sweden have resorted to similar measures, some even offering negative interest rates. These actions of Central Banks have *force fed demand*. Savers have been punished by these non existent interest rates and have been forced to take on more risk in search of yield.

What has transpired since has allowed the world's economies to reflate. Most major governments have systematically devalued their currencies and taken on more debt in the process. Governments, through their asset purchase and bond buying programs, have created straw buyers. This false demand created by governments who have acquired assets over the past decade has been artificially manufactured and has distorted prices to all time and *bubblicious* highs.

The Fed's hope is that they can now *normalize* by raising interest rates, and withdrawing their phony demand without negatively upsetting the capital markets. I do not believe that is likely.

Before explaining why, let's first look at the three main areas where debt has been incurred, measure the overall debt growth/ contraction over the past decade, and then evaluate how this has impacted asset values up to this point. From there we can look forward and make some educated guesses on what is most likely to occur next.

14 EVERYBODY'S DOING IT

"If your friend jumped off a bridge, would you do that too?"

Moms everywhere

A Trillion Here, A Trillion There, What's the Difference?

Today the total global debt stands at roughly $220 Trillion and has *tripled* in 17 years. Government debt has ballooned to $63 Trillion, with the U.S. making up roughly a third of all of that debt. Corporate debt globally stands at $65 Trillion, and consumer debt is roughly $90 Trillion worldwide. We are literally **swimming** in debt. Everett Dirksen was a senator in the 1960's who famously said "A billion here, a billion there and pretty soon we are talking about real money." Who could have imagined that only 50 years later that we would have the same indifference? Only now billions would have turned to trillions.

If debt growth is like a cancer cell that grows until it ultimately kills, the sheer growth alone over the past 18 years indicates this cancer is a major problem to our future health. If we have any chance of future survival we must find ways to reduce this overall debt, or cut it out altogether. Sovereign governments who take on massive debts they cannot repay must ultimately resort to devaluation of their currencies.

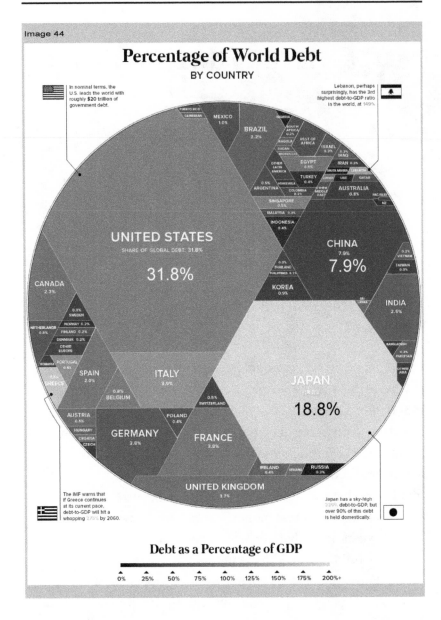

Debt is defined by Webster as, "money that is owed or due." In order for a debt to incur there must be two parties; the *borrower* and the *lender*. The *cost* for money is determined by *interest rates*. It is the interest rate that the lender expects to receive *plus* its principal which becomes the incentive to the lender (usually the bank) for making the transaction. For the borrower, the incentive is to pull forward *future earnings* to afford *today* what he would otherwise need to wait to purchase.

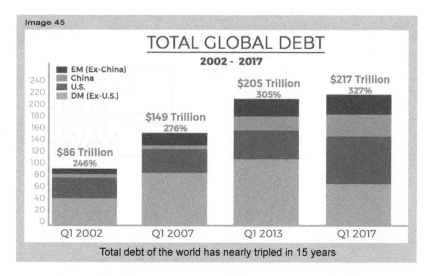

Image 45

TOTAL GLOBAL DEBT
2002 - 2017

- EM (Ex-China)
- China
- U.S.
- DM (Ex-U.S.)

$86 Trillion
246%

$149 Trillion
276%

$205 Trillion
305%

$217 Trillion
327%

| Q1 2002 | Q1 2007 | Q1 2013 | Q1 2017 |

Total debt of the world has nearly tripled in 15 years

This is a natural tool for most people. If we all needed to wait to buy a car or a home until we could afford it there would be a whole lot less people doing these things. Taking on debt allows us to afford today, what we will earn tomorrow. For this to work the borrower naturally needs to pay the lender back not only the principle, but also the interest due. If the borrower cannot afford to pay the lender back there will be loss, or worse default.

Debt without growth leads to loss or defaults. This is so powerful it needs to be reiterated. **Debt without growth leads to loss or defaults.**

Sovereign Debt Explosion

The United States has gone from roughly $10 Trillion in debt in 2008 to over $20 Trillion in debt in 2017, less than a decade later. How on earth will we pay for all of this? The obvious answer to this simple question is that we cannot and will not ever pay the debt off. The best we can hope for would be that we could, one day, manage to pay it down. With the current debt-happy political landscape, (as evidenced by the most recent tax bill that will openly add another $1.5 Trillion to the national debt), the odds are excellent that the national debt will surge higher, not lower, in the coming years. From here there is only one way out: devalue the dollar and pay our debts with our continually watered down currency.

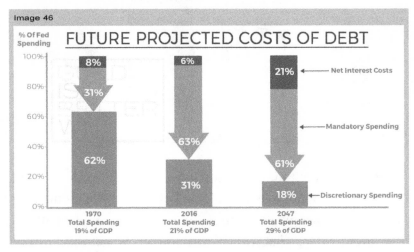

Deficit spending is growing and not shrinking. Mandatory spending programs are growing even faster. Taxes are being lowered. Military and infrastructure expenditures are increasing. Is anyone thinking about how we will pay for all of this?

Notice that interest payments on our debt are set to consume a major portion of our future expenditures up from 6% today to over 21% in the next 30 years. The additional costs for servicing debt will actually eclipse government spending allocated to discretionary programs. Not only will we be forced to devalue the currency by printing more money, we will likely also be forced to dramatically cut discretionary spending in the future.

15 **WHO CARES?**

"Don't worry about stealing people's ideas. If they're any good you'll have to ram them down people's throats"

Howard Allen

Debt Matters And Nobody Seems To Care

When economies don't grow on par with their debt, they are eventually forced to devalue their currencies in order to sustain an ever growing debt burden and pay down debt with *diluted* dollars. In this way, governments don't necessarily default like individuals or corporations do. Instead, governments devalue their currencies.

Since the Bretton Woods agreement in 1944, the U.S. Dollar has been the world's trading currency. The United States has been in the enviable position of being able to devalue our currency without ever defaulting. This will work until it doesn't. Ever since The Federal Reserve was created in 1913 The Fed has been devaluing the dollar. In fact, The Fed has devalued the dollar by 96% in that time.

This has been accomplished by manipulation of interest rates and controlling the money supply. Lowering interest rates is the first step in this scheme. It allows for debt to be accrued at a lower service cost.

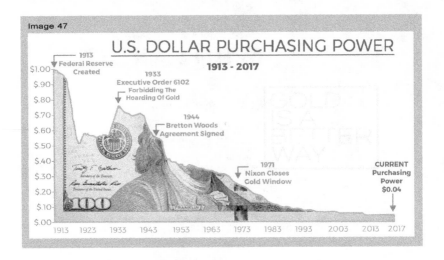

Image 47

- From 1913 to 1971 an increase of $400 Billion in federal debt cost $35 Billion in additional annual interest payments *(9% of that total debt)*
- From 1971 to 1981 an increase of $600 Billion in federal debt cost $108 Billion in additional annual interest payments *(16% of that total debt)*
- From 1981 to 1997 an increase of $4.4 Trillion cost $224 Billion in additional annual interest payments *(5% of that total debt)*
- From 1997 to 2017 an increase of $15.2 Trillion cost "just" $132 Billion in additional annual interest payments *(Less than 1% of this additional debt!!!)*

The five phases of my personal student debt example can be seen occurring here as the U.S. Government takes on more and more debt that costs less and less to service.

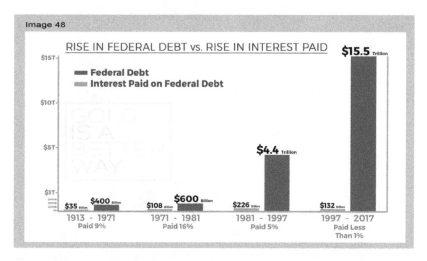

Image 48

RISE IN FEDERAL DEBT vs. RISE IN INTEREST PAID

- Federal Debt
- Interest Paid on Federal Debt

$15.5 Trillion

$4.4 Trillion

$35 Billion $400 Billion $108 Billion $600 Billion $226 Billion $132 Billion

| 1913 - 1971 | 1971 - 1981 | 1981 - 1997 | 1997 - 2017 |
| Paid 9% | Paid 16% | Paid 5% | Paid Less Than 1% |

Phase One: Debt Appears The Same As Demand

In the 18 years from 1981 to 1998, the national debt of the United States expanded nearly eight times. This explosion in debt was fueled as interest rates went lower from 20% down to 3%. This is akin to my early college experience when I was continually able to take on more debt through more credit cards. The initial explosion of debt appears as demand and prices rise as credit expands.

Phase Two: Debt Is Allowed To Grow As Interest Rates Are Lowered

Precisely in correlation with my own personal debt experience, when I initially paid my credit cards on time and then was offered more credit at better rates, the U.S. has been able to sustain massive debt growth over the past 20 years via progressively lower and lower interest rates. As we have taken on more debt, the costs to service it all have gone down, providing a false sense that our house is in order. This technically allowed our dollar to become stronger from 2012 to 2016 while we added an *additional $5 Trillion in debt.*

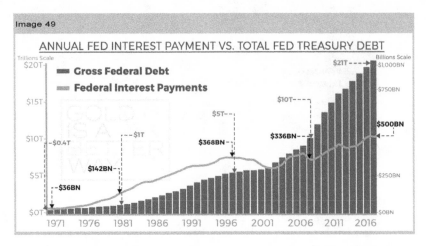

Image 49

ANNUAL FED INTEREST PAYMENT VS. TOTAL FED TREASURY DEBT

Image 49 shows this visually. Notice that our debt just continues to climb and our costs have moved laterally. We are at a tipping point, however, as at this moment costs are about to surge higher as interest rates move higher.

Phase Three: Credit Tightens

Global credit will tighten and interest rates will move higher. This will force higher debt service costs and lead to decreased spending, which is happening now. Notice that the costs to service our debt are flat and actually came down from 2012 to 2015. The costs to service our debt since the end of 2015 have been going higher and will continue to from here, in a dramatic way, as deficits continue to increase and interest rates go higher.

Phase Four: Consumption Decreases

Tightening credit caused a change in my demand and consumption. Coming soon to countries everywhere.

Phase Five: Default

Debt burdens become too great, leading to austerity and default. The United States is about to enter into Phases 4 and 5 in the next several years.

Consider the five phases:

1. Debt has exploded in the last 20 years.
2. Our additional *costs to service* all of this debt have *decreased* or remained flat as we have taken on more debt because of ultra low interest rates.
3. This debt explosion has driven asset values to current levels as this debt has fueled that demand.
4. Housing, stocks and bonds have all been massively inflated by these lower interest rate policies.
5. Debt service growth is at a tipping point. The future costs of the existing debt will likely surge higher from here as deficits expand and interest rates continue higher.

GOLDEN NUGGET # 5
"Things that make you go "Hmmm…""
I wouldn't buy gold either!

The most widely held ETF tracking the gold miners is GDX. Notice GDX is down 41%, while gold is up more than 2.5X!

Do the calculation yourself. Go to www.goldisabetterway.com

The ETF tracking junior miners is down 60%, while physical gold is up 20%!

Image 51

GDXJ			PHYSICAL GOLD			
START	END	% CHANGE	START	END	CHANGE	%CHANGE
107.12	33.55	-69.61%	$1,087.50	$1,314.88	$227.38	20.91%

$30,386.48 $120,908.51

	INVESTMENT	START 01/01/2010
	$ 100,000	END 05/01/2018

Do the calculation yourself. Go to www.goldisabetterway.com

If you have a 401k or a company sponsored retirement plan, the best option you may have is to invest in gold is the Tocqueville Gold Fund. TGLDX is down 20% over the last 12 years, while physical gold is up over 150%!

Do the calculation yourself. Go to www.goldisabetterway.com

16 STEROIDS

"We didn't have steroids back then. If I wanted to get pumped up, I drank a case of beer"

Art Donovan

Corporate Debt - All Pumped Up

Wall Street has consumed a massive amount of debt steroids. These actions have allowed corporate America to *juice* their short-term performances. Wall Street has borrowed $3 Trillion for free. The boom has been a sight to watch and, for now, everyone is happy. But at what long term expense? Corporate America borrowed money for free and then, rather than invest in their employees and infrastructure, they've bought back their stocks. This corporate borrowing has driven equity valuations into the stratosphere. Taking advantage of the low interest rate environment has been a huge gift for equity owners as their shareholder value has increased 300% since 2009 when they last bottomed out.

Any baseball fan will remember the early 2000's. America's national pastime was transformed into a totally different game before our eyes. Baseball had forever been a game of defense and strategy, but it morphed into one of constant offense and scoring. This was because players started hitting more home runs. A lot more.

Slammin Sammy Sosa, The Bash Brothers (Mark McGuire and Jose Canseco), and baseball's superman Barry Bonds became household names. They excited fans by launching glorious home runs further and more frequently than anyone in the history of the game. Madison Avenue made these guys even more famous as they spawned advertising catchphrases like *"Chicks dig the long ball,"* a major marketing campaign for Nike at the time.

What was happening in baseball? Players that had averaged 20 home runs a year were now hitting 35. Players that had been averaging 30 home runs were now hitting 50. And the few mentioned above, (Sosa, McGuire, Bonds), who had averaged 40 home runs previously were now hitting more than 60 to 70 home runs in a season! In 2001, Barry Bonds launched a previously inconceivable 73 home runs.

This home run total crushed a former Major League Baseball record of season high 61 home runs recorded by Roger Maris that had stood for 37 years. Even the most famous home run hitter in history, Babe Ruth, had never hit more than 60 home runs in a season. The Babe's 60th homer stood as a record in baseball for 38 years. Now in the same decade, three players, (Bonds, Sosa and McGuire), all eclipsed this nearly impossible feat.

At first it was thought that maybe the baseball was being designed differently and that Major League Baseball was *juicing* the ball in an effort to create excitement through higher scoring games. It seemed everyone was hitting the ball further. Another theory was that these professional athletes were beginning to train year round and had become more specialized in their crafts at an earlier age. Whatever the reason, the fans loved it. Baseball's popularity, which had been declining in the 1990's, was on the rise again.

We now know that it wasn't the ball that was juiced. It turns out it was the athletes themselves. Steroids were liquid power. The home runs they generated sparked a new enthusiasm among fans of Major League Baseball. These incredible Hulk-like specimens it turns out were not Greek god descendants. They were cheaters. And overnight when their steroid use became public, our heroes became zeroes.

What did these steroids they ingested do? Steroids permitted athletes to *pull forward* greater strength than that which could otherwise be achieved naturally. Steroids allow athletes faster recovery times and to heal more quickly. The long term effects of steroid use can create horrible future health consequences. Athletes stole from their *future health to pull their performance forward.*

In 2007 the scandal came to light and Major League Baseball was forced to change the way they tested athletes, committing to efforts to eliminate steroids from the sport. The guys who had been popping dozens more home runs per year when taking steroids, now hit home run totals back in line with their historical averages. Once the steroids were removed the players went from superhuman back to normal. The excuse used by some of the athletes that cheated was that *everyone was doing it* and had they not, they wouldn't have been able to compete.

Steroids Are To Athletes What Debt Is To Corporations

Steroids did for the game of baseball what *debt* has done for the stock market. When *debt steroids* are removed from the market, it will likely have a similar effect. The markets will revert back to their historical valuations and investors will lose trillions as this occurs.

The comparison of debt to steroids is remarkable. Today, debt allows corporations to *pull forward* future performance. Just like steroids allowed players to hit more home runs *in the present.* Debt allows for *explosive short term* results in rising share prices when it's consumed in the present in the form of stock buybacks.

Debt can have the future crippling health effect on growth. Debt, like steroids, can have a negative long-term health effect on corporations that rely on it. Just like steroids made baseball more exciting, debt has brought a new excitement to the game of investing as everyone likes to see more home runs in the form of higher and higher indexes.

Finally, when all is said and done, the excuses of our corporations who binged on debt to inflate their stock performance will be the exact same as athletes that inflated their performance via steroids. They will say 'we *needed* to borrow money and buy-back shares in order to compete.' In other words, *everyone was doing it* and in order to compete, we needed to as well.

When the free money party is over, when borrowing costs increase and when CEO's can no longer afford to buy back stock or pay off all of this borrowed money, what will happen? The borrowing binges will end, corporate performance will return to the fundamentals of earnings and profits, and the markets will deflate as numbers return to normal. The companies we see as heroes because of their recent eye popping performance may become zeros as their stocks sink. What will CEO's say then?

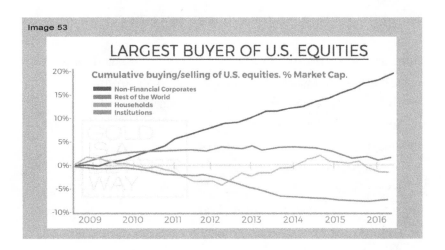

Image 53

LARGEST BUYER OF U.S. EQUITIES

Cumulative buying/selling of U.S. equities. % Market Cap.

Non-Financial Corporates
Rest of the World
Households
Institutions

Buying back shares and there by inflating share prices is a strategy they will argue was in the best interest of their stockholders. In the short term this may have been true, in the long term it will not.

Expecting the same performance in the future, after access to this free money has been taken away, is akin to removing steroids from the game of baseball and expecting players to hit as many home runs. It ain't gonna happen.

The bad news for investors is that Central Banks are doing just that; taking the steroids away and raising rates. As they do the value of stocks and bonds will decrease. If you own equities, the overall performance of your portfolio could suffer greatly, just like Major League home run hitter's performances deteriorated greatly after the artificial juice had been taken away. We have already begun to see this take place in one major sector of the economy.

17 THE NAKED TRUTH

"I told my wife the truth. I told her I was seeing a psychiatrist. Then she told me the truth: she was seeing a psychiatrist, two plumbers, and a bartender"

Rodney Dangerfield

The Retail Story

By now we are all aware of the Amazon Effect. With its online platform, Amazon is able to deliver products to anyone, virtually anywhere within days, sometimes even hours. These products come directly to the door of the consumer. It's fantastic for buyers who now never have to leave their home to purchase products that they need and want. Amazon has put big pressure on retailers.

Brick and mortar businesses are losing market share and facing big headwinds as more and more shoppers flock to the convenience and lower prices offered by Amazon. Macy's, Sears, JC Penny, J Crew, Forever 21, Wal-Mart, Target and dozens of other retailers are closing stores by the hundreds, and bankruptcies are surging. Amazon is winning and it's at the expense of traditional retail.

While this pressure is certainly very real, it's not the biggest challenge retailers are facing. The big problem actually *preceded* this shift into online shopping.

The root cause of the issue occurred decades before as investors poured money into commercial real estate. That commercial real estate demand got the attention of venture capital. It launched the birth of big box and other large stores in nearly every category from suppliers like Staples, Sam's Club, and Best Buy, and Toys "R" Us. The result of this commercial real estate boom was far too much capacity, too many stores, too much square footage of space, and all of it in a rapidly changing environment.

That boom is now going bust. The sharp needle popping this bubble is the *inability* of retailers to *service their debt*. Nearly 7,000 stores were shuttered in 2017. 550 department stores closed, accounting for over 43 million square feet of space. How did this get so bad? Follow the money for your answer.

After the financial crisis in 2008 Wall Street set its sights on retail. With interest rates at 0%, Wall Street convinced major retailers to take on massive amounts of debt in the form of corporate bonds. It was free after all. Retailers had a leverageable asset: real estate. The idea was simple. Borrow money practically for free and then use those dollars to increase value for shareholders and corporate executives by buying back stock. Everybody wins and this works, until it doesn't. Much of the debt maturity on these retail bonds was 7 to 10 years.

This debt is now hitting maturity, and could be disastrous timing. While many industries have struggled since the great recession, retail has been among the hardest hit due to a cultural change in the way people now shop. Today more people shop online than at anytime in history. 2017 is projected to be the first year where Christmas shoppers purchase more online than in physical locations.

Debt Without Growth Leads To Default

Retailers are not growing, they are slowing down. The costs to service all of their debt is becoming due at the worst time. Their debt and the costs to service it are becoming unmanageable at the exact moment that profits are shrinking. Amazon's prices, have also forced margins lower equating to less profits for the traditional retailers. This all spells bad news for retail.

What may be a sign of the beginning of the end for retail is their inability to find new lenders willing to roll over their debt. At a time when institutional bond buyers have been lining up everywhere in a hunt for yield, retail is having difficulty finding new money to borrow. Offering higher interest rates that far exceed what bond buyers can find anywhere else hasn't helped. Retail is having big problems rolling over their debt.

Much of retail has entered phases four and five of the debt cycle. Phase Four has found them closing stores at unseen rates. Phase five has seen outright default on debt.

Zombie Companies

The case of Toys "R" Us exemplifies the pressure facing retail. The toy company was founded in 1948 and over time became the predominant brand in retail toys. They eventually expanded into Babies "R" Us and Kids "R" Us. At its peak they were considered a *category killer,* so powerful and efficient that they pushed every other retailer out of this specialty space. They became one of the most famous brands in all of the United States and Canada.

In the wake of the financial crisis, and after several years when the toy company had been losing market share, they took on a very large amount of debt. Toys "R" Us would continue to lose market share to Amazon and other online retailers over the past decade. The financial crisis and the subsequent zero interest rate environment were actually a savior of sorts for the company. This environment allowed for the toy company that was already dying, to stay afloat. They continually took advantage of further borrowing and restructuring of their debt.

Toys "R" Us finally buckled under its crushing debt load. Inability to find new lenders toppled the retailer in a matter of days in September 2017. The toy company was unable to restructure $400 Million in borrowings due in 2018. The speed of their downfall was reflected in their bond values that traded at par in the beginning of September and plunged to just 18% of face value three weeks later. The overall debt of Toys "R" Us is roughly $5 Billion, under which the toy company had been operating for nearly a decade. Their annual costs on their debt of $400 Million became too deep a burden as their sales declined into rising costs. They filed for Chapter 11 Bankruptcy in 2017.

What happened to Toys "R" Us is also happening right now across a large portion of retail and many other sectors of the economy across the country. Wall Street feasted on retail and other zombie entities after the financial crisis. Bankers made large fees for providing these corporations with capital and the spigot was turned on for nearly a decade. In the short term everyone won as Wall Street banks made huge fees, and CEO's and shareholders saw their share prices surge higher.

In the long run, *without the necessary investments to spur growth* that would support all of the outstanding debt, corporations will be forced into restructuring their debt to pennies on the dollar or to outright default causing debilitating losses for bondholders.

There is another way this could have gone. Rather than use debt to fund share buybacks and financially engineer stock prices higher, retailers could have invested those borrowed dollars into building their own online platforms that could have given Amazon a run for their money. In fact, retailers were in a far better position to capitalize. They, at one time, had more ability to engage with their own loyal customers and built-in audience. Instead, rather than *invest* in infrastructure and better online platforms, retail *consumed* that debt and are now finding this diet of easy money has sped up their own demise. What has happened in retail is emblematic of what has taken place across a much broader swath of corporate America. Zombie companies have overindulged on cheap money.

Wall Street's Goodfellas

All of this reminds me of a scene from the movie *Goodfellas*. Goodfellas is a film about a group of mobsters in New York, starring Joe Pesci and Robert De Niro, directed by Martin Scorsese. Pesci and De Niro are mobsters who have gone into business with a local restaurant/bar owner. At first the owner benefits as the mobsters fleece the business. They purchase everything on credit with no intention of paying. Liquor, steaks, and other supplies acquired on credit come in the front door and then immediately go right out the back door to be sold on the black market for pennies on the dollar. The mobsters and the owner all share in the proceeds from the black market sales. All of this revenue is *profit* because they have zero intention of paying the vendors who have fronted (loaned) the inventory.

The mobsters continue this scheme of taking in borrowed supplies in the front door and then selling them on the black market. The farce grinds to a halt when they cannot find any more suppliers willing to provide credit and front the inventory. When this occurs, rather than pay off the debts owed to vendors, the mobsters burn down the restaurant and take the insurance money. As he watches his beloved business burning, the restaurant owner with tears in his eyes says, "This used to be a great business."

The *Goodfellas* of Wall Street have provided corporations with the ability to stay alive and thrive in the short term. Corporations have continued to binge on borrowed money just like the Goodfellas from the movie. More loans at lower rates that fleece the future for the benefit of today.

In a free market society, where money was not free and bankers were not forced to lend, the story would likely be different. By manipulating interest rates to these extreme low levels The Fed has encouraged bad behavior from Wall Street and put a big dent in what was formerly known as Capitalism.

Junk

A junk bond is simply riskier corporate debt. AAA rated firms can borrow at a better rate than firms with shakier credit. Companies with less than perfect credit ratings can borrow money, it's just more expensive. Lenders naturally demand a higher yield for taking on riskier debt. This is no different than an individual with a perfect credit history getting a better rate from a lender than a subprime borrower.

Central Banks have manipulated interest rates to absurdly low levels. Like a crack cocaine dealer handing out free samples, this free money has enabled zombie companies to take on debt that otherwise without which they would be unable to survive. The ability to take on more debt has kept theses zombies alive and they became addicted to it. This has created risk premiums that are deeply out of whack for bond investors.

As bond lenders across the globe seek yield, bond prices have driven higher and higher. Less attention than ever is being paid to the subprime corporates *ability to repay* as more focus has been on *seeking yield*. This has forced lenders into taking more risk than they otherwise would in a more normal environment.

The historical average yield for *subprime* corporate debt has ranged between 12-15%. As investors have hunted for yield, that price is now closer to 4% for U.S. subprime corporations. It's even worse in Europe where junk rates have fallen to under 3% and *junk* is more expensive than anytime in history.

This effectively means that investors are taking larger risks than ever before in order to drive returns in this environment. Are investors being compensated accordingly?

Evidence is overwhelming that capital is flowing from out of Europe and Japan, and into the U.S. credit markets as interest rates turn negative overseas. Why? Is this flow of capital due to some booming excitement about the U.S. economy and how well we are doing here? Sadly not. The answer is far more simple: this is money that has nowhere else to go.

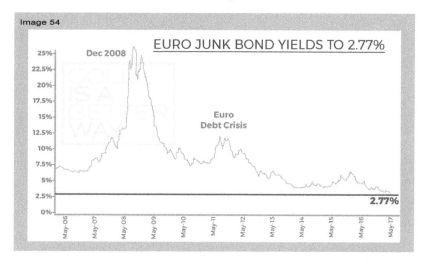

It would certainly appear that investors are not being compensated for their risks appropriately. As capital lending requirements tighten and costs to borrow increase in the coming months and years, corporations who have managed to survive due to low rates will find that rolling over their debt and borrowing new money will become more difficult. As a result, more and more businesses will fail. This cannot end well for investors. It is a main reason why many economists have pinpointed the junk bond markets as a potential epicenter of the next global financial crisis.

Should interest rates surge higher, as is the stated goal of The Fed, look out for serious carnage in the junk bond markets. To make all of this worse, everyone is looking for the exact same signals. When these signals come into full view there could be a rush to the exit doors.

18 THE LITTLE GUY

*"I used to be in a little debt and it bothered me a lot, now
I'm in a lot of debt and it just bothers me a little"*

Tim Clue

Somebody Has To Lose

One of the immediate and positive reactions after the financial
crisis was seen in the consumer debt space and their activity.
Unlike governments and corporations, individual consumers in
the wake of the financial crisis actually deleveraged. Consumers
dramatically reduced their consumption, began saving, and
lowered their overall debt burdens.

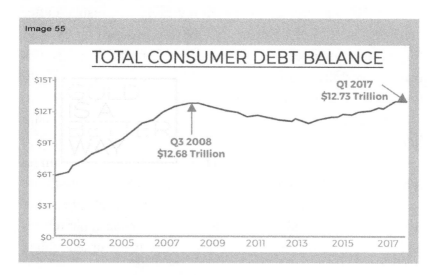

Image 55

TOTAL CONSUMER DEBT BALANCE

Q1 2017
$12.73 Trillion

Q3 2008
$12.68 Trillion

After the financial crisis, consumer debt balances went lower. Much of this was predicated by the fact that banks were not freely lending to the consumer. Consumer credit tightened in 2008 as lending standards towards consumers became rigid. This lack of liquidity forced the consumer to tighten their belts and live more within their means. Savings rates of consumers went up from 2008 to 2012 while credit tightened. This has reversed since 2012 and consumer credit is now at all time highs.

Housing

The initial tighter consumer standards were felt most deeply in housing. Banks demanded much better fundamentals from their borrowers and required a larger percentage of the home price to be deposited as a down payment. Mortgage lenders were also requiring much higher credit scores to approve loans for their borrowers. These actions have created a new dynamic in the real estate sector.

Rather than making individual loans for home buyers, mortgage lenders were mostly lending to conglomerates, private equity, and Real Estate Investment Trusts (REITS) after the housing crisis. A large portion of the cheap inventory that resulted after housing lost 40% of its value in 2008 was scooped up by Wall Street conglomerates. The percentage of inventory of homes owned has shifted more heavily to the groups that were able to take advantage of the loose money floating around in the system. Wall Street corporations now hold an unprecedented ownership in housing stock.

Wall Street giants like Blackstone now own millions of single family homes. New corporate buyers have boxed out first time homebuyers who don't have access to the same levels of capital. This transition has led to a much larger share of consumer renters as opposed to home buyers. These former buyers turned renters are chasing less and less rental inventory and this has spurred rising rents across the country.

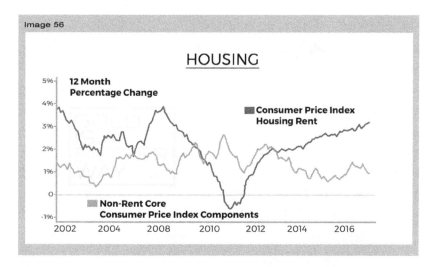

This is among the inflationary pressures facing Americans. The core Consumer Price Index (CPI), which does not include rental inflation, is just above 1%. Rent inflation has driven upwards to almost 4% annually. To make matters worse for the consumer, just as mortgage lending standards began loosening for everyday first time home buyers in 2015, home prices have risen so significantly due to Wall Street's gobbling up of inventory that home ownership, which at one point epitomized the American dream, will remain just that for most first time home buyers; a dream.

In October 2017, the price of new homes had never been higher and was growing at a much faster pace than incomes. A simple look at the trend in housing highlights the great divide taking place between the wealthy and the poor. The little guy was encouraged by Wall Street to take on bad loans from 2004 to 2007. These were loans that Wall Street knew borrowers couldn't afford. When housing prices imploded individuals suffered massive losses. Then Wall Street swooped in a bought up all the inventory at pennies on the dollar.

After the bubble popped, it was not the little guy that was able to capitalize on the deflated home prices. Mortgage loans were not made available to them. Only now, after home prices are finally back at all time highs, are banks willing to lend to the little guy again.

Subprime Autos

Unlike the housing market which saw a considerable tightening in consumer credit after the financial crisis, the credit offered for new and used car buyers, especially in sub-prime loans, skyrocketed after 2009. The reason is simple to understand. With interest rates so incredibly low, and bond investors on a hunt for yield, the subprime automobile sector became the go to for the Wall Street bond bulls.

Access to a personal vehicle is among the largest necessities for adult Americans. The demand for auto ownership has been among the steadiest consumer demands as it is so vital. The car is our conduit to work, school, shopping, and the everyday activities that Americans share. For people with shaky credit their best option may be to borrow on the subprime markets with high interest rates and hefty fees. These loans have a habit of haunting people as debt collectors will continue collections long after the cars have been repossessed. Many Americans still find themselves paying for cars they don't even own anymore.

This has been a good thing for Wall Street and bondholders who have repackaged these subprime loans into securities. Very similarly to the housing bubble, many of these auto loans have been consumed by individuals who cannot afford them. Rising interest rates make it even more costly for car buyers. Lending standards, which had been incredibly loose in the car industry, are now tightening as interest rates inch higher. This will only further pressure car borrowers as more of their disposable income will be directed toward paying off debt than toward new consumption. It will come as no surprise that delinquencies spiked to 10 year highs in subprime auto loans in 2017.

Student Loans

The student loan bubble may be the number one threat facing the United States and is indicative of the massive challenges facing our economy. The costs of higher education have literally ballooned. The amount of debt outstanding adds up to $1.4 Trillion. **This is higher than the total dollar amount of subprime mortgages that sparked the financial crisis.**

Ingrained in the psyche of Americans, who still believe in the *American Dream*, is the notion that a college degree is essential to one's ability to find success in the world. High school seniors are pushed into getting degrees from higher education. The only way for many to afford college is to borrow. We are pushing our youth to take on serious debts for long periods of time. The availability of student loans makes it relatively easy to pay for college. Although all types of debt have been on the rise in the last several years, student loan debts have increased at a dramatic rate. Unfortunately, graduates are not making enough money to handle the burdens of all the debt they take on. An alarming 11% of all student debt was delinquent or in default in early 2017. The student loan bubble encompasses an enormous amount of debt that millennials carry.

We are looking to millennials to keep the economy going. Two major consequences will arise for our economy as a result of this bubble.

There will be massive defaults on these loans since median incomes are not rising anywhere near the increased costs of higher education. Perhaps more important to the future strength of the economy, millennials who can be expected to buy cars

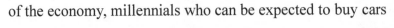

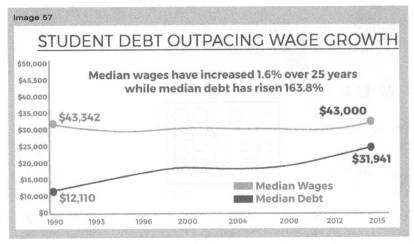

Image 57

STUDENT DEBT OUTPACING WAGE GROWTH

Median wages have increased 1.6% over 25 years while median debt has risen 163.8%

$43,342

$43,000

$31,941

$12,110

■ Median Wages
■ Median Debt

1990 1993 1996 2000 2004 2008 2012 2015

$50,000 $45,500 $40,000 $35,000 $30,000 $25,000 $20,000 $15,000 $10,000 $0

and homes and other consumer goods that drive the future of the economy will not be able to afford them. Unlike a car loan or a home loan which can be wiped clean via bankruptcy, student debt cannot be walked away from.

This is already evidenced in the way that millennials are acting thrifty and staying away from credit card debt. The pressures this puts on the future of the economy are hard to measure. It's logical to expect that all of this debt burden will put pressure on this demographic to start their own side businesses and second jobs in addition to working 9 to 5 jobs to pay down their existing debt obligations.

More than likely, this student loan bubble will require deep restructuring. Since the vast majority of these loans are government backed, the final burden will fall on the taxpayer. We must understand that all of this debt overhang puts a tremendous stress on the future of the world economy.

Warren Buffett's father was among the biggest gold bugs in history and fought adamantly for staying on the gold standard and fought to restore it while he was a Congressman for 10 years

Warren Buffett's father, Howard Homan Buffett, was an Omaha stockbroker and four term Republican Congressman from the state of Nebraska.

Buffett's father gave the following impassioned plea when warning of the great the hazards that would most assuredly befall the United States if we went off the gold standard:

"I warn you that politicians of both parties will oppose the restoration of gold, although they may outwardly seem in favor of it, unless you are willing to surrender your children and your country to galloping inflation, war and slavery, then this cause demands your support. For if human liberty is to survive in America we must battle to restore honest money. There is no more important challenge facing us than this issue. The restoration of your freedom to secure gold in exchange for the fruits of your labors."

Additionally Buffett's father would argue "paper money systems generally collapse and result in economic chaos."

IV

WHAT COMES NEXT

19 PASSIVE INVESTING

"Sitting still can become a pain in the ass"

Milton Berle

Weapons of Mass Destruction

In the aftermath of the financial crisis in 2008 Warren Buffett famously called credit default swaps *weapons of mass destruction*. Some experts are pointing out that Exchange Traded Funds (ETF's) may be the financial instrument that is most responsible when the everything bubble finally pops. These *buy everything* ETF's have distorted stock prices and created huge potential for risk should this bull turn into a bear.

There has been a tremendous amount of publicity surrounding the huge amount of capital flowing out of hedge funds and managed accounts and into passive index funds. Index funds can be a better way for the average investor due to the lower cost structure compared to actively managed funds.

Why? The *fees* charged by hedge funds can be as high as 2% per year and 20% of the gains. This puts massive pressure on the overall performance. These fees, when compounded over time, can eat away at the overall gain for the investor. Even active managers who charge a 1% fee will struggle to compete with index funds whose cost structure may be as much as 60% less.

A deeper look reveals what may pose as the greatest risk to our markets from this point forward. In an environment when virtually *all* stocks have gone higher, owning an index fund has been the best way to maximize performance. Central Bank policies have lifted all boats... up until now. There are massive risks inherent in these index funds.

1. Lack Of Price Discovery

When buying the whole index, an investor is exposing themselves to all companies as opposed to ones with the best fundamentals. We have some exceptional corporations in our country that have promise and upside potential for future growth. At the same time we also have companies that have managed to stay afloat, binging on debt, whose futures are far from certain. An index fund cares little about fundamentals as ALL companies are acquired. The result is that all boats get lifted in bull markets.

When an announcement is made that a company is being added to the S&P 500, its stock price typically jumps about 10%. The fundamentals are exactly the same, but because its now been added to the index and passive index funds will be buying them, these stocks are then immediately worth more. Passive index demand drives all prices higher.

There are also many excellent companies that have great balance sheets and strong fundamentals whose share prices are handicapped because they do not trade within the index. In fact, it is one of the great dilemmas facing strong, non indexed or private companies. Because of passive investing, their share prices may not rise in correlation with their fundamental strength.

2. How the Index Is Weighted

The bigger the company, the bigger its weight in the benchmark, relative to other stocks. This leaves investors more vulnerable to bubbles which will inevitably burst. In 1999, at the height of the Internet craze, technology stocks made up roughly 30% of the S&P 500. By 2002, tech stocks made up just 14% of the index. Today that number is roughly 25% and FAANG, along with Apple, make up 10.6% of the index.

In the event of a selloff, FAANG stocks can get hit the hardest because so many investors hold passive index funds. On August 20th, 2017, we saw this exact situation transpire. While the overall index was down roughly 1.5%, FAANG stocks dropped 5% in one day. In other words, the biggest weighted players benefit most when everyone is buying the index, and can get hit hardest when widespread selling occurs. Their weight in the index makes them more appealing in a bull market and less appealing in a bear market.

3. What Happens When Everyone Wants To Sell?

So much has been made about why we are in a bubble. The Fed, by lowering interest rates to 0%, forced investors searching for yield out of fixed investments and into the equity markets. But interest rates will not be zero forever. As interest rates rise it will put pressure on the overall market as money flows away from riskier assets like stocks and into other assets that can bring a safer and more meaningful yield.

Should interest rates spike quickly, this could mark a large sell off in the markets. In this environment it's not hard to see how all corporations will be hurt as investors flee these funds. If buying everything helps passive index funds outperform active manager gains on the way up, selling everything will speed up the pain on the way down.

4. Buy Everything

One of the other reasons passive investing has so greatly out performed active is that passive deploys *all* capital and is always fully invested. Active managers will often have a portion in cash to deploy when assets drop in value. That lack of cash may create the biggest challenge of all. If everyone is completely invested, who will be left to buy when selling occurs? Where will the cash come from? In fact, one of the biggest risks resulting from the growth in passive investing is the potential lack of liquidity. The next downturn will likely get exacerbated as selling begets more selling as buyers will have less cash available to purchase.

20 IT COULD GET MUCH WORSE

"My prediction? Pain!"

Clubber Lang - Rocky III

What Could Go Wrong?

While a strong case has been made for the future price of gold based on our nation's debt and future debt affordability, prompting a future price projection of $2,600 within the next three to four years, the price of gold could explode much higher. Should a crisis occur, the following are the most obvious potential crises laying in wait:

1. Pension Fund Crisis

A pension fund is a retirement plan whereby the employer makes contributions into a pool of funds set aside for the employee's future benefit. That pool of funds is then invested on the worker's behalf in order to generate income for the employee in retirement. At the end of employment the final amount of accrued funds is available to the worker in a lump sum or monthly payments. Retirement projections are dependent on how well the underlying investments in the plan perform. Pension computations are performed by actuaries using assumptions about demographics, life expectancy, future levels of tax contribution and investment returns. As of right now, pension funds are underfunded by an estimated $4 Trillion.

Employees who have worked their entire lives expecting guaranteed income during retirement may ultimately find that there are in fact no guarantees. This is a not a *far off in the future* problem. This is happening *today*. State and local governments continue to underestimate the problem. Not only are we $4 Trillion in the hole, unfunded liabilities will likely get worse.

The actuaries that calculate the necessary minimum returns for pension funds to grow according to schedule have factored in a 7% annualized return. It is the fundamental math that must occur for these plans to be viable. With interest rates on the floor, pension fund managers have been forced to take more risks than ever before as they search for yield. These funds are under tremendous pressure to meet this 7% return threshold. Pension fund obligations far outweigh the money they are bringing in and the money they have in reserve. This presents a near impossible challenge for pension fund managers and bodes horribly for the future retirement hopes of millions of Americans who are expecting pension payments to support them through their retirements.

It's all about the math. The massive pension fund losses in 2001, and then again in 2008, wiped out big portions of fund assets. Actuaries made their models on *consistent* market returns and did not factor in colossal losses as part of the projection.

Retired employees are also living longer and are receiving benefits longer. This is occurring simultaneously as a shortage of new contributing employees are entering the workforce to offset these payment imbalances.

The actuarial models of 7% returns were created in the 1980's and 1990's when investment returns of this level were the norm. It has become increasingly more difficult for fund managers running these pensions to achieve returns near that 7% average. The pension crisis is a giant elephant in the room that everyone can see but nobody seems to be taking any efforts to address. The biggest challenge is that if pension funds were to adjust their rates of return lower, these funds would require additional funding today. States are unwilling to adjust their models as it would require higher taxes, the agreement to which is politically infeasible.

For pensions to have any chance of hitting their projected numbers, it requires that equity returns, and other alternatives, continue to grow as dramatically as they have in the last few years. The consistent buying of equities by pension funds that have nowhere else to go has been one of the major catalysts to the stock market's dizzying growth. Traditionally pension funds have allocated much of their capital across less risky bond funds. As interest rates fell of the cliff, these funds have been forced to take on more risk by flowing into the equity markets. This flow has been a further support that has helped the stock market hit new all time highs almost daily in 2017 and has forced valuations to extreme levels.

This pension crisis is a slow moving Titanic that is headed for an iceberg of lower returns for longer periods of time. Eventually, pension funds across the country will go bankrupt unless returns dramatically outperform the 7% return models, or elderly pensioners begin dying more rapidly. Neither seems very likely.

The more likely solution is that taxes will need to go higher or these municipalities will go bust. Public sector bankruptcy is a markedly different animal than corporate default. When a corporation goes bankrupt a court will ultimately decide how the remainder of the corporate assets get divided. This is not the same in a public bankruptcy. Since the primary asset of a city or state is the future tax revenue, citizens can ultimately walk away and move. High tax states like New Jersey, Illinois and New York, are experiencing firsthand migration herds as people are moving away to lower tax areas in the Midwest and The South. Nearly twice as many people moved away from New Jersey, New York and Illinois as have moved into those states in the past 5 years. This migration has been fueled by a search for the states with the lowest tax structures, such as Nevada and Arizona who have benefited greatly from this migration.

How will all this end? Will individuals keep migrating to avoid higher local taxation? And if they do, won't that put even more pressure on the states receiving these people for state provided services and thereafter tax increases in these receiver states? What happens if more and more pensioners choose a lump sum over monthly payments? What money, if any at all, will be left for the current employees expecting these same benefits when they retire? The pension system is a ponzi scheme that requires incoming money to pay the money outgoing. If large lump sums are withdrawn at once rather than over time, won't this put even more additional pressure on this underfunded mess?

How this ends as a whole is not an exercise in prognostication. This is an exercise in logic - future retirees will be left with less, not more. The connection between *making ends meet* will get further and further apart. Pensions will lose value and require bailing out.

Those bailouts will be funded through printed money and devalued currencies here in the United States and around the world. The future living standards of retirees will be far worse and workers will be forced to work far longer.

2. Declining Reputation Of America - Don't Blame Trump

For the last 74 years, the United States of America has enjoyed one of the greatest home field advantages in history. After establishing the U.S. Dollar as the world's reserve currency, every other country in the world has had to follow our lead. The value of the U.S. Dollar has had a massive impact on the economies of the rest of the world during this time.

The dollar is backed by the *full faith and credit* of the United States. Much of this book has been dedicated to how that credit, which for the longest time has managed to uphold around the globe, is now at the tipping point of a serious decline. Budget deficits and debt affordability are two of the main reasons why our credit rating as a country will inevitably decline in the next several years, and in a very serious way. The U.S. has been in deep decline since the turn of the century. This is an ongoing and long-term build up of what happens when countries take on far more debt than reasonable. Don't blame Trump, but do be aware.

What doesn't get discussed enough is the *faith* part of that equation. Our legislature has become a machine at odds with itself. Ideas are immediately dismissed, regardless of merit, by the opposing political party. The democratic process that allowed for our nation to rise above all others no longer exists. What is in the best interest of the people, which our elected officials are sworn to uphold, is disregarded along party lines and the ability to find compromise within our government system has disappeared.

Behind a country's wealth and success are the policies that create opportunities, and people that shape the perspective and environment. Having an aggressive and combative President, while perhaps effective in certain ways, leaves America in a position of *us versus them.* Instead of looking for areas of agreement with other nations, our current nationalistic approach may only cause further divide.

Trump is often compared to Ronald Reagan. They both are in favor of business and against big government. They both looked to make business-friendly, pro-growth changes to the tax code. They both believe in expanding the military. Comparing the two men in this way is a fundamental basis for the high hopes amongst Republicans who voted for Donald Trump. What's perhaps the most ironic aspect of this comparison is the main agenda that both men may be remembered for. In 1987, in one of the most famous speeches ever made by an American President, Ronald Reagan commanded the leader of the Soviet Union, Mikhail Gorbachev, to **"tear down this wall"** referring to the Berlin wall that separated East and West Germany. By contrast, as evidenced by throngs of supporters shouts during the 2016 Presidential Campaign, Trump ran on a platform of separation. '**Build that wall**' referring to the wall Trump promised to build between the United States and Mexico became an identifying label of the Trump movement, ('Lock her up' was a close second).

The world has become an embittered and angry place. This is less the fault of Donald Trump and more emblematic of the frustrations many feel around the globe. It has led to nationalistic agendas. The United States has already backed away from NATO. America has also pulled out of the Trans Pacific Partnership, and has threatened to leave The North American Free Trade Agreement (NAFTA). Whether this ultimately leads to better or worse deals for our country will only be known in time. What is evident is that these positions polarize the United States in position and, more importantly, in image. We were known as a country that had other nations backs, earning us the title of policeman of the world. Now we may be seen as the bully in the playground, taking aggressive positions and taunting our neighbors through rhetoric that divides rather than unifies.

The enemy of my enemy is my friend is a concept that has stood the test of time. No longer do enemies of our enemies fear being *beaten up* by the big brother, the United States. An area of concern is that our aggressive and nationalistic posture may actually drive our enemies closer together, making us their agreed upon opponent.

Our political system, once the envy of the world and arguably a primary reason for the emergence of America as a world superpower, has disintegrated into a broken machine. That machine has ground to a halt. Increased polarization and bipartisanship has pushed sides further apart. Our political system no longer works for the greater good. It now works for one side or the other. That it works at all for one side is enough and often the only reason it doesn't work for the other.

The inability to find compromise amongst our elected officials prohibits prosperity in ways that have become obvious to the rest of the world. The image of the United States, that at one time served as the land of excellence, opportunity and freedom, has degenerated into more an image of incompetency. Favorability ratings from around the world have plunged over the last twenty years.

The purpose of this book is not to take a political stand, but rather to highlight the impact of fundamentals that have led us to this juncture, and how they will impact the future value of financial assets as well as the future values of gold and the dollar. What can get lost in this evaluation, which is based exclusively on numbers, is that *faith* is not measurable. *Faith, by definition, is confidence in things unseen.*

While putting America first sounds like it should be positive for the United States, that egoism has been a factor that has directly challenged our reputation around the world. While taking a strong and unbendable stand in negotiations may be an effective strategy in business, taking similar unbendable positions in diplomacy with other nations can be cause for strife, conflict, and perhaps even war.

Our reputation matters, especially when thinking about the future strength, or existence at all of the U.S. Dollar. Putting America first may push other countries closer together and allow for trade to occur without the use of the dollar at all. Dollar supremacy is continually challenged. The rise of digital currencies like Bitcoin are additional evidence and cause for serious concern about the long term viability of King Dollar. Viability that, once lost, could forever alter the current wealth of the United States and all of our citizens. Should that faith be lost, the dollar could collapse and gold would then soar to unseen heights.

3. Global Demographics

Earlier we discussed the largely positive impacts that demographics and the birth of the baby boom generation had on the growth of asset values on the U.S. economy. This demographic explosion was not unique to the United States. While the U.S. population has doubled over the past 50 years, the population of China went from 600 million people in 1950 to 2.5 times that amount at near 1.5 billion people today.

Factoring in demographics and how they impact the future growth is fundamental to understanding where we are headed, and how that may impact the future of financial assets that have been fueled by debt. **A primary argument of the book is that debt without growth leads to loss or default.**

The demographic growth in world population that has been supportive of asset values over the past 50 years will now become a major headwind over the next 50 years as the population growth rate is expected to decline significantly.

Further tilting the future balance away from growth is the fact that human beings are living an average of five years longer than 50 years ago. This means more people are leaving the workforce than ever before, and these people live longer, needing additional support from entitlement programs like Social Security, Medicare, Medicaid, and other social programs.

Bloated entitlement programs are a major issue for governments and for the future ability to pay down the debts that have been accumulated the world over. It's no surprise that the largest block of voters, the baby boomers, have elected representatives that continue to prolong and extend these underfunded programs that are beneficial to them individually, and will have profound negative impacts on the futures of their children and grandchildren. Many have argued that the baby boomers and their egoistic agendas, which have been carried out by politicians needing their votes, are among the primary reasons we are in so much debt today. Their gain and standard of living will be passed on to their heirs with more pain and strife. The boomers will be the first generation that leaves their heirs worse off than their parents did.

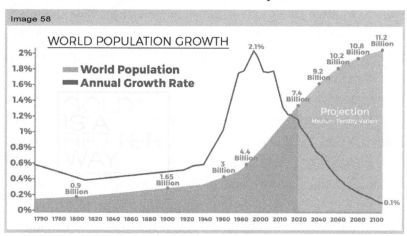

When looking at the future demographic projections the world population witnessed a radical uptrend from 1900 to 1960. This uptrend naturally led to greater growth. From 2020 to 2100 world population growth is expected to radically decline. This decline in the human population would appear to be a big headwind for long term growth.

4. Required Minimum Distributions

10,000 people **per day** will turn 70.5 between now and the year 2035. The flow of retirees funds may be another massive headwind for asset values forging ahead. When there are more buyers than sellers asset values increase. What happens when there are more sellers than buyers? Asset values go down.

As retirees draw down on their retirement accounts to live on, they will be forced to sell more of their holdings as they increase in age. The rules of IRA's, which currently hold over $18 Trillion in assets, require retirees to sell a percentage of their portfolio each year, starting when they turn 70.5 years old.

These people are not only living longer, they will also be forced to sell a portion of their holdings. The IRS requires mandatory annual distributions from qualified retirement accounts each and every year after 70.5 years of age. The first of the baby boomers were required to take distributions in 2017. Over the next 18 years there will be a tsunami of sellers that will grow exponentially year after year.

Unfortunately, an issue shared by pension funds is also evident within retirement accounts. That issue for the equity markets in general is that the Y and Millennial generations will not have the same capacity to invest as their parents and grandparents did in the stock markets. More and more of our younger generations incomes will be forced to go towards paying off the debts incurred by their parents and grandparents. Since the markets are made up of buyers and sellers, the next 15 years will see far more sellers leaving the market than buyers entering.

Another alarming fact is that millennials, a generation of greater size than baby boomers, are putting less and less money into the equity markets. They've witnessed their parents and grandparents suffer through the dotcom bubble, and then the collapse after the housing bubble. As a result they are less inclined as a generation to invest in similar ways to generations prior. This is not a good sign for traditional paper investments like stocks and bonds, and may ultimately bode quite well for cryptocurrencies and other alternative assets that are outside the system.

GOLDEN NUGGET # 7

Things that make you go "Hmmm..."

How Much Is A Trillion Anyway?

Close your eyes for a moment and try and imagine a trillion of anything. A million is perhaps something we can wrap our minds around.

A billion? That's a little bit more challenging.

A trillion dollars? Hard to conceive.

Let's think about it a different way. Guess how long one million seconds equals?

11 days.

Try guessing how long a billion seconds is?

32 years.

Take a guess how long a trillion seconds is?

32,000 years!

When we are talking about trillions of dollars we are talking impossibly large numbers that are virtually impossible for the normal mind to conceive.

V

GOLD PRICE $10,000 PER OUNCE

21 REASONS IT COULD GET *VERY* UGLY

"Give a man a match and he will be warm for a minute.
Set him on fire and he will be warm for the rest of his
life"

George Carlin

Gold $10,000 Per Ounce And HIGHER

My prediction for gold to double to $2,600 per ounce over the next three to four years is strictly based on the depth of understanding I have about how debt works and the headwinds facing the world economy in the coming years. I believe I have made a strong case for gold to double fundamentally simply based on the United States rising costs to service our national debt.

Actual Fair Value Of Gold Today

What is the fair value of gold today? In 2008 our country's national debt hit $10 Trillion. At the time gold was more fairly valued, in my opinion, and priced at $1,000 per ounce. Since that time we have tripled the money supply and doubled our country's total debt to $20 Trillion. When combining this, my calculations add up to six to seven times more overall money supply through credit and new money creation that existed just a decade ago. If gold was more fairly valued a decade ago when it was $1,000 per ounce, and we have multiplied the overall supply of new money creation, the fair value of gold today should be between $6,000 and $7,000 per ounce.

By taking cycles that play out where commodities return to their fair value in the coming years into account, and then adding to that the additional and necessary devaluation that comes from rising costs to service global debt obligations, I believe you will see gold somewhere north of $10,000 over the next 10 to 12 years. **This means by the time we get to 2030, I believe we will see gold prices north of $10,000 per ounce.** If I am correct, in order for the Dow to keep pace it would need to rise to 200,000 points in the same period of time.

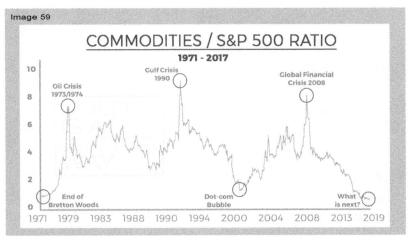

Image 59

COMMODITIES / S&P 500 RATIO
1971 - 2017

Recall the equity to commodity ratio discussed earlier. I point out once again that commodities are at a position in the cycle where they historically outperform equities on an 8:1 ratio from current levels. For my thesis to be accurate, cycles will continue as they similarly have in the past. In 1973 the price of gold was $100 per ounce. Seven years later gold would rise to $800 per ounce. In 2000 the price of gold was $240 per ounce and would rise $1,925 in 2011. Each of these increases amounted to 8X. Gold rising to $10,000 per ounce would mark an 8X rise from its current price levels

I am not alone in making this projection of gold $10,000 per ounce. Gold expert Jim Rickards believes that gold will hit $10,000 per ounce. As stated in his book *The New Case For Gold*. Rickards comes to this price by looking at the base M1 money supply with gold at a fair backing of 40%.

Leigh Goehring is a world famous commodity trader who has been investing in commodities since the early 1980's. His Wall Street career has been exclusively devoted to understanding and investing in oil, gas, precious metals and other commodities. In 2000 his firm predicted gold would go to $2,500 per ounce. He was wrong, but not by much. Gold rose from $250 per ounce to $1,900 per ounce a decade later. Any investor that bought gold at these levels and sold near its highs was rewarded with large returns.

In a 2018 interview with Real Vision TV, Goehring lays the case for why he believes gold will rise from current levels to $13,000 per ounce. He argues that gold is actually one notch below levels it was in 2000, based on the overall money supply in the system. It was the overall level of supply that allowed his firm to quite accurately predict the massive run up in gold from 2000, and it's the same methodology he and his firm are using to predict the coming super spike in gold.

Twelve years may seem like a long time. Gold could most certainly surge to this price level sooner. Every assumption I make about the future price of gold is based on the U.S. Dollar continuing to be the world's trading currency, from which all major currencies still peg themselves.

There are five main reasons why gold could surge dramatically higher than my $2,500 per ounce estimate in the next few years. I will not spend too much time delving into any of these potentialities. This is not because they are unlikely to happen. It's mostly because I believe these to be self evident. My purpose is to highlight why I believe gold is a better way without the typical doomsday scenarios. It is my certain belief that gold will provide a far better option than any other asset classes in the coming years. That said, it is important to highlight some of the more obvious reasons why it is more essential to own gold now than any other time in history.

1. War

Perhaps the very number one reason to own physical gold now more than anytime in recent history is the current threat of war. War can take many forms and can be a hot war, a trade war, or even a cyber war. The most obvious and immediate reaction to a serious military conflict, especially one that includes detonation of nuclear missiles and loss of millions of lives would be dramatic. It seems that the odds of a significant hot war includes nuclear war have increased significantly in the last year. The rhetoric employed by President Trump aimed at North Korea's Kim Jung Un is enough to make anyone who understands history very nervous. The markets have completely ignored this possibility. Should this worst case scenario occur, expect financial assets to plummet globally while physical, tangible assets explode higher. None are likely to surge higher more than physical gold.

2. Financial Crisis

We are only a decade removed from the last financial crisis. I have spent a great amount of time highlighting the bubbles and therefore extreme risks that investors have been pushed into taking since that time. The challenging thing about predicting a financial crisis is that nobody knows where the next one will come from or how bad it could ultimately be. We will assuredly have a recession in the coming years. The real unknown is if Central Banks will have the tools available to keep us out of the abyss when that transpires? Should the world's population lose faith in Central Banks there will need to be a complete restructuring of the monetary system. I believe that anyone who owns physical gold in this scenario will be in the best position to capitalize, while everyone without will suffer severe paper losses.

3. China

China has its own set of issues related to debt exposure. It is essential to highlight that China has much stronger growth prospects than the United States. China is an aggressive acquirer of physical gold and many believe that is in preparation to be in position to make the rules in a new world order. China is the world's largest consumer of oil. It has a population of 1.4 billion people, which is 1 billion more than the United States. The growth that China is going through will allow them to continue to become a stronger player on the world's stage in the coming years. They have begun taking active measures for this inevitability. In 2015, after years of being denied, the IMF made China and the Renminbi an official part of their special drawing rights (SDR) basket. This will allow China to see roughly $2 to $3 Trillion of inflows into the Renminbi over the next 7 to 10 years, according to Morgan Stanley. China is actively pursuing opening a gold window, and tying their currency to gold. This would allow for them to purchase oil in their own currency versus doing that in U.S. Dollars, thus providing oil suppliers from the Middle East further confidence to do business outside of the U.S. Dollar.

4. Debt To GDP Ratio

Perhaps the most important number to look at for the long term is the U.S. Debt to GDP Ratio. Every major superpower in history that had a fiat currency, whose Debt/GDP exceeded 100%, soon thereafter ceased to be a superpower. Currently our debt is 103% of our total GDP. We are over $20 Trillion in debt, with a GDP of about $19 Trillion. This is a clear and present danger for the long term future of the U.S. Dollar.

5. Paper Gold

While many individuals own physical gold around the world, especially outside the United States, it is estimated that the amount of outstanding paper contracts meant to be backed by gold are leveraged anywhere in excess of 50 to 1. While this has not been an issue up until now as the system for trading paper gold has held up nicely, this could shift dramatically in a crisis. Should more people holding gold contracts attempt to redeem them than supplies allow for, it is logical to expect that paper gold and their holders could see that value plummet while physical holders of gold see the value of their holdings surge, perhaps exponentially.

22 DIGITAL GOLD

"If you want something real, stop entertaining temporary things"

Anonymous

Digital Currencies and Gold

The rise of Bitcoin and other digital currencies has led to a passionate debate about the worthiness of these currencies as an asset class. The meteoric rise in the price of Bitcoin in 2017 brought tremendous heat to the crypto space. Dozens of new coins have been minted and adopted by investors and traders and there are hundreds of billions of dollars of market capitalization and investment devoted to this burgeoning industry. The awareness has been explosive and feels to many like a mania. Investors that are students of history will point out that these parabolic moves higher in the price of any asset, like Tulips in 1636 to 1637 and dotcoms in the late 1990's are a result of investor euphoria and bullishness that is indicative of late cycle behavior.

When it comes to digital currencies there are definitely a lot more questions than answers at this point. What are digital currencies really? Are they payment systems or an asset class? What is their utility? Is the technology sustainable as massive amounts of energy are required to produce new coins? Are they safe and secure and can these systems be trusted. Will governments regulate them, tax them differently or attempt to eliminate them altogether by making their ownership illegal? How can an asset backed by a new technology be trusted to last, when technological improvements are constantly being made, whereby new technologies render older ones obsolete?

While the answers to these questions will play out over time, what is clearly obvious in the moment is that there is a deep allure to digital currencies. I believe it's valuable to consider *why* there is such strong interest in digital currencies and then look at where the demand is coming from; millennials.

Many famous and intelligent investors have called digital currencies a ponzi scheme and that these coins will all be worthless at some point. I believe that there is a deep interest in currencies outside the system of the current Central Bank manipulated structures. That interest can be measured when looking at where the demand for these digital currencies comes from. A recent poll by Blockchain Capital indicated that more than 33% of all millennials would prefer to invest in digital currencies rather than in stocks and bonds. That same poll found that more than 70% of millennials are aware of Bitcoin.

This millennial awareness, coupled with the fact that this is a massive demographic that's hitting their peak earning years, warrants consideration for the future value of Bitcoin and other digital currencies. Much like the baby boomers who drove stocks higher and higher in the 1980's and 1990's as they hit their peak earning years and then invested in the stock market, millennials who are now looking to invest may choose Bitcoin and other digital currencies over the next 20 years.

Ultimately, multiple digital currencies have the same issues that multiple paper currencies have, and will need a static standard by which all can be measured. This is why I believe it will not be long before we have digital currencies backed by gold. The combination makes too much sense. There will always be those that mistrust digital assets due to the lack of tangibility. Digital transactions make up the vast majority of all financial transactions today and it looks like a trend that will only further continue. By combining the liquidity and speed of digital with the safety, security, and non-manipulability of physical gold, gold-backed digital currencies would become impossible to ignore. It makes sense that these new offerings will develop in the very near term and outside of the Central Bank's design. As new digital currencies backed by gold become more accepted, the demand for physical stores of gold will increase and drive the price of physical gold significantly higher.

Future Of Central Banks

All of this brings up an important consideration: where will Central Banks fit in should this all occur? As mentioned, Central Banks, including the IMF, hold roughly 25,000 tons of gold. As gold backed crypto-currencies are developed and adopted, this overwhelming supply could allow Central Banks a deep advantage in determining the rules and structure of a new digital monetary system backed by gold. I believe the most likely future scenario is one where the current monetary system ultimately collapses sometime within the next 10 to 15 years. That collapse will likely come after a deep depression and a populist movement and uprising. That movement will naturally be led by millennials. When the transition to a new world order and monetary system eventually occurs, it seems reasonable to assume that the world will share a universal currency that is digital. I believe that digital one-world currency will be backed by gold.

In the end I believe that gold, the element that was the basis of the monetary system for thousands of years, will outshine all others. Should this all play out according to my prediction it would be reasonable to assume gold prices of $25,000 per ounce, or even higher, in order to accommodate the need for appropriately inflating the value of gold to support a new world monetary system.

23   A NEW STRATEGY

"If you must play, decide upon the three things at the start: the rules of the game, the stakes, and the quitting time"

Chinese Proverb

The Game Is Changing

Imagine you were invited by some of your friends to go to the local park to throw the ball around a little, maybe even get a small flag football game going. You think to yourself, "I may not be in the best shape of my life but, hey, I'm still a pretty good athlete and hope the old form will be there just like it was, maybe just a little rusty." It's a beautiful Saturday afternoon, and it would be great to see some of your old pals, so you say, "Why not?" and decide you'll join.

When you arrive at the park you see some of your friends and start tossing around the football. In between throws you manage to get in a few side bends and leg stretches to limber up the body. Sure enough, just as you expected, after a few minutes your form starts to come back and you think to yourself, "I've still got it!" Your buddies are also feeling the same, and what started as a lighthearted ball toss is now becoming a bit more competitive. Guys are running actual pass routes as others are trying to defend.

You take a step back and marvel that, even though you are all in your mid 40's, the gang looks pretty good. Soon someone breaks out the flag belts and it's time to pick teams.

As captains are being decided on, you see a new face show up. He seems to be walking with a purpose right towards you. You can tell that this guy has a plan just by the way he says hello. It turns out it's Bill Belichick, the future Hall of Fame coach of the New England Patriots. He has seen you and your mates warming up and is wondering if you may be interested in playing a little game with some of his friends? On cue, as if this experience hadn't been cool enough, the "guys" Coach Belichick points to are the actual New England Patriots. There is an army of young men in the greatest shape of their lives wearing Patriots T-Shirts and are all walking towards your crew. Wow, this is incredible! Sure enough, standing right there before you is arguably the greatest quarterback of all time, Tom Brady. As he extends his hand, he smiles and says, "Hi, I'm Tom, hope you will play some football with us."

You and your friend's minds are blown. You can see most of them trying to keep their cool as if this kind of thing happens every day, and yet a few can't resist getting out their cameras to take selfies with Brady. Your wife is never going to believe this! After a few autographs and hi-fives it's time to play.

The teams are going to be you and your mates versus the New England Patriots. Everyone is wearing flags around their waists, and you think, "Wow, this is going to be so awesome."

Brady has the ball and you find yourself covering Rob Gronkowski, the All-Pro Tight End. You think to yourself, I sure hope my buddy Joe has the video camera rolling because nobody is going to believe this. Brady lobs the ball 'back shoulder left' to The Gronk. But you can see the play developing, and just as you always could spot an easy opportunity, you plant your right foot and drive your momentum right in front of Gronkowski and intercept the ball in full stride.

A feeling of elation enters your whole spirit as you can imagine the stories you're going to be telling for the rest of your life about how you intercepted the actual Tom Brady. In a split second you're daydreaming about all of your future Thanksgiving dinners where you will be recounting this incredible moment in your life to your in-laws.

But now that you have the ball, it's time to score! So you start getting the legs going, and they begin to fire like pistons. Not only are you going to pick off Tom Brady, you're going to take it to the house! As you make your way down the sideline you can hear the ESPN highlight jingle, "Da-da-da, da-da-dum, da-da-dum!"

Just as you are envisioning the touchdown dance you're going to do once you hit the end zone, (your famous version of The Electric Slide that always gets a huge laugh and round of applause), you hear a loud roar that wakes you from your dream state. Bearing down, just five yards behind you is a wide-eyed, angry 22 year old, 325 pound lineman who is way faster than you, and this guy looks serious. Soon you find yourself overcome with downright fear and your legs, which just a moment ago were firing on all cylinders, now feel like they have cinder blocks for shoes. You think to yourself *this is just a friendly game, I'm sure this guy won't actually tackle me.* That hope is almost immediately dashed as you see Brady himself charging at you from a different angle as he yells, "Crush him!" to his huge lineman.

Fear has turned to terror as you find yourself getting obliterated. It's literally like being hit by a truck that's moving 25 miles per hour. The only difference is this truck has arms the size of tree trunks and, while he hits you full force like a heat seeking missile, his massive arms simultaneously squeeze around your pot belly of a stomach as all of the air you have ever breathed seems to get sucked out of you in an instant. The once-friendly Tom Brady piles on as you hit the ground, adding a left forearm shiver to the side of your neck that makes you feel like your head will pop off. As you go down and pain shoots through your nervous system from all sides, when you think it couldn't get any worse, you hear Brady whispering in your ear, "Oh, you wanna play huh?"

You look up to see that all of your buddies now have a completely different look on their faces. They are all terrified. Their prior childlike looks of awe and exuberance are now replaced with a much different look: fear.

Belichick extends his hand to help you up and says, "Nice play. Now let's have some fun and play for real." Thankfully you're still alive and although your body may never work the right way ever again, your brain function has never been more acute. You offer a feeble, "That's okay, I think we've had enough fun for one day" and can see all of your buddies nodding in agreement. You offer your hand to say thanks for the fun and it's completely ignored. Belichick puts the ball on the line and says, "Your ball, 1st down."

Despite all of your attempts to quit the game you find you cannot. You and your friends, who were just coming out for a nice weekend football toss, now find yourself in a game of life or death playing against **professionals** who are faster, stronger, smarter and better than you in every way. It's a losing proposition. The best you can do at this point is try to survive, because there is no way to win. You are stuck and the only way out is to go through it. You can guarantee one thing: even if you somehow survive, you are going to walk away from this game badly injured.

This entire scenario sounds ridiculous, right? It's outrageous to think that a professional sports team would ever consider playing in this kind of game. Certainly nobody in their right mind who was not a professional would ever willingly agree to be engaged in a battle this lopsided. Who on earth would even dare put themselves in this kind of harm's way knowing the inevitable outcome? Who would ever agree to a game without first knowing the rules? Who would ever dare to risk so much against opposition that so clearly has the upper hand? Who would ever think playing in this kind of environment would be a sound strategy? The answer is obvious: no one.

And yet this is **exactly** what most of us are doing with our *investments*. Aren't we all playing against **professionals** who are far smarter, stronger, and faster than we are? As retail investors we are competing with *professionals,* against whom we are no match. These players are moving massive amounts of capital at speeds we cannot even conceive much less compete against. Unlike Tom Brady, who would never act this way, these very real market players entire goal is to win at all costs, no matter who gets hurt. In fact, in this game, your loss is their gain.

The game we are all playing is changing. This is a fact most of us are either unaware of, or are unwilling to accept. If we did, we would assuredly either stop playing altogether, or at least change our current strategies to match the new rules of the game.

We must become aware that the playing field is not level and the players we are facing have tremendous advantages of power, speed and information that we do not have, nor will we ever possess. Unlike the professional athletes from my made up scenario, who may out of kindness and fairness take it easy on you, the players we are facing in the markets are playing a **zero sum game**.

Until we realize that the only way to win a race against a faster opponent is to start running way before they do, or not race them at all, we will forever be playing a game where we have very little chance of winning. This is a game that if we play too long will injure us terribly or eliminate us altogether.

There Are No More Little Guys....

The game didn't used to look like this. In the mid 1980's, the vast majority of all of the money in the stock and bond markets was allocated by *individual retail* investors like you and me. The remaining money was made up of institutional investors. These figures have now completely reversed.

Today, 90% of the money in the markets is controlled by institutional investors. These hedge funds, pension funds, sovereign wealth funds, and investment banks are moving massive amounts of capital faster than any retail investor is able. This massive pool of money gets information that you don't, and they get it faster.

We have all been told by the experts that you cannot *time* the markets. They tell us that the only way to win is to buy and hold and *stay the course*. At one time, when interest rates averaged 7% and we had steady growth, a buy and hold was a sound strategy. When markets go up over time, and continue to do so, staying the course makes all the sense in the world. In the boom and bust markets we've experienced since the turn of the century, *staying the course* has been a good strategy. *Get the heck off the course* would be a good strategy when or before, the markets collapse.

There is a famous saying goes, "When you sit down at a poker table and cannot identify the sucker, the sucker is likely you." Imagine you're sitting at a poker table with 10 players. You are playing with your entire nest egg of several hundred thousand dollars. To your left are five guys playing with hundred million dollar stacks. The four guys to your right are playing with stacks in the billions of dollars. They all know each other, they know the dealer, and they have far more information about how the deck is stacked than you ever will.

Lately the investment game as been akin to playing poker with a lot of aces in the deck. Everyone can have fun and win. This is a good description of our markets over the last eight years. Money printing and interest rate manipulation has made everyone winners as stocks and bonds have all gone higher.

But the game is changing, *literally.* Central Banks are telling us they will be **tightening monetary policy** and interest rates are expected to rise in the coming years. As these events occur, bubbles will be popped and investors who have enjoyed the unprecedented easy gains that Central Banks helped create will see them greatly diminished if they do not change their strategy.

Conditions Matter

If I am traveling to Hawaii I probably want to pack a lot of bathing suits and light clothing, not a lot of scarves and sweaters. If I am traveling to Alaska I probably need less light clothing and more heavy overcoats. The environment will dictate the proper attire I need to pack in order to best deal with the elements.

Wall Street won't advise you that a changing environment requires a change in strategy. I will. Interest rates are changing. The Federal Reserve is forecasting four rate hikes in 2018, following the four rate hikes that began in December 2015. This is a huge environmental shift. You need to change your strategy, and you need to do it now.

As the financial environment changes from warm to cold you will want adjust your investment strategy. Fewer bathing suits, more sweaters. Defensive positions like commodities, gold, and cash will best shield you from the elements on the horizon.

24   FINAL WORDS OF WISDOM

"If not now, when?"

Adam Baratta

It's Time To Take Action

Too often as investors we are focused on the second hand of the clock when we actually should be aware of the time. We are in a late cycle economy that is over-leveraged, facing inflationary pressures, and suffering from slow growth. Financial assets will underperform from this point forward and tangible assets and commodities will surge. If you want to prepare yourself to win, there is only one thing left to do...

Buy gold now.

GOLDEN NUGGET # 8
Things that make you go "Hmmm..."

You're Golden - It's Inside You

Did you know that you actually have gold in your cells?

96% of the human body is composed of the elements Oxygen, Carbon, Hydrogen and Nitrogen. The other 4% consists of other elements. We absorb small amounts of gold from our environment and gold is present in our cells at birth.

The average person's body weight is 154 pounds and contains 0.229 milligrams of gold.

If it were possible to extract this amount of gold from our bodies it would only be worth about $11 at today's spot price of $1,296 per ounce.

Scientist Neil Degrasse Tyson explains this phenomenon in a poetic way: "Many people look up at the stars in the sky and its expanse and feel small because the Universe is so vast. I look at the Universe in a different way," he says, "I understand that the Universe was created from an incredible explosion of matter. We, as human beings are part of that matter. When I look at the Universe I realize that it is inside of me - the stars and the elements that make up its matter are inside of me and rather than feel small, I feel vast."

Gold. It's in you.

Selected Sources

Abramowicz, L. (2017, December 08). Vanguard's Bogle Sees Pension Pain: 'It Will End Badly'. Retrieved from https://www.newsmax.com/finance/streettalk/vanguard-jack-bogle-pension-bond/2017/12/07/id/830598/?ns_mail_uid=96163743&ns_mail_job=1768035_12082017&s=al&dkt_nbr=01012449crnk

An Update to the Budget and Economic Outlook: 2017 to 2027. (2018, April 09). Retrieved from https://www.cbo.gov/publication/52801

B. (2017, September 05). Reduction In The Rate Of Growth Of Federal Income Tax Revenues (Article 2 Of 10). Retrieved from https://seekingalpha.com/article/4104075-reduction-rate-growth-federal-income-tax-revenues-article-2-10

B. (2017, September 07). Increasing Federal Medicare And Social Security Entitlement Costs And Debt (Article 3 Of 10). Retrieved from https://seekingalpha.com/article/4104784-increasing-federal-medicare-social-security-entitlement-costs-debt-article-3-10

B. (2017, September 08). The Growing Federal Annual Budget Deficit, And Projected Cumulative Debt (Article 4 Of 10). Retrieved from https://seekingalpha.com/article/4105241-growing-federal-annual-budget-deficit-projected-cumulative-debt-article-4-10

B. (2017, September 11). The State Pension Funding Crisis Will Likely Result In Pension Benefit Cuts (Article 5 Of 10). Retrieved from https://seekingalpha.com/article/4105695-state-pension-funding-crisis-will-likely-result-pension-benefit-cuts-article-5-10

B. (2017, September 12). Individuals Will Face Slow Wage (And Jobs) Growth, Hence Limited GDP And Discretionary Income Growth (Article 6 Of 10). Retrieved from https://seekingalpha.com/article/4105976-individuals-will-face-slow-wage-jobs-growth-hence-limited-gdp-discretionary-income-growth

B. (2017, September 13). The Coming Retirement Savings And Income Crisis (Article 7 Of 10). Retrieved from https://seekingalpha.com/article/4106414-coming-retirement-savings-income-crisis-article-7-10

B. (2017, September 14). Record Household Debt Limits GDP Growth Going Forward (Article 8 Of 10). Retrieved from https://seekingalpha.com/article/4106868-record-household-debt-limits-gdp-growth-going-forward-article-8-10

B. (2017, September 17). Increasing Healthcare And Other Costs (Article 9 Of 10). Retrieved from https://seekingalpha.com/article/4107479-increasing-healthcare-costs-article-9-10

B. (2017, September 18). A Future Of Slow GDP Growth, High Federal Debt, And Strained Household Finances (Article 10 Of 10). Retrieved from https://seekingalpha.com/article/4107622-future-slow-gdp-growth-high-federal-debt-strained-household-finances-article-10-10?page=2

BA, A. B., & Zulfiqar, M. (2017, September 13). The Buffett Indicator Is Sending Investors a Dire Warning. Retrieved from https://www.lombardiletter.com/the-buffett-indicator-is-sending-investors-a-dire-warning/17248/

Beck, T. (2017, April 9). Bond God Jeff Gundlach Is Essentially Long Gold. Retrieved from https://www.streetwisereports.com/article/2017/04/09/bond-god-jeff-gundlach-is-essentially-long-gold.html

Brill, J. (2018, January 25). A New 'Bubble' Warning. Retrieved from https://stansberryresearch.com/articles/a-new-bubble-warning

Brown, K. (2017, November 19). How to Spot a Market Top. Retrieved from https://www.wsj.com/articles/is-this-the-top-of-the-market-1510856195

Buffett, W. (1998, February 27). BERKSHIRE HATHAWAY INC. 1997 Chairman's Letter . Retrieved from http://www.berkshirehathaway.com/letters/1997.html

Carr, D. (n.d.). FDR's 1933 Gold Confiscation was a Bailout of the Federal Reserve Bank. Retrieved from http://www.moonlightmint.com/bailout.htm
Cartwright, M. (2014, April 04). Gold in Antiquity. Retrieved from https://www.ancient.eu/gold/

Cheng, E. (2017, May 12). Manager of the world's biggest hedge fund says the long-term economic picture 'looks scary'. Retrieved from https://www.cnbc.com/2017/05/12/ray-dalio-says-the-long-term-economic-picture-looks-scary.html

Corkery, M., & Cowley, S. (2017, May 17). Household Debt Makes a Come-back in the U.S. Retrieved from https://www.nytimes.com/2017/05/17/business/dealbook/household-debt-united-states.html

deGrasse Tyson, Neil. "A Quote by Neil DeGrasse Tyson." Goodreads, Goodreads, www.goodreads.com/author/quotes/12855.Neil_deGrasse_Tyson.

DePersio, G. (2017, October 23). How Do Asset Bubbles Cause Recessions? Retrieved from https://www.investopedia.com/articles/investing/082515/how-do-asset-bubbles-cause-recessions.asp

Desjardins, J. (2017, November 06). Infographic: $63 Trillion of World Debt in One Visualization. Retrieved from http://www.visualcapitalist.com/63-trillion-world-debt-one-visualization/

Durden, T. (2015, November 12). The Amazing Chart Showing What All The Debt Issued This Century Has Been Used For. Retrieved from https://www.zerohedge.com/news/2015-11-12/amazing-chart-showing-what-all-debt-is-sued-21st-century-has-been-used

Durden, T. (2017, April 4). The Next Subprime Crisis Is Here: 12 Signs That The US Auto Industry's Day Of Reckoning Has Arrived. Retrieved from https://www.zerohedge.com/news/2017-04-04/next-subprime-crisis-here-12-signs-us-auto-industrys-day-reckoning-has-arrived

Durden, T. (2017, August 17). Carmageddon: Deep Subprime Auto Delinquencies Spike To 10-Year Highs. Retrieved from https://www.zerohedge.com/news/2017-08-16/carmageddon-deep-subprime-auto-delinquencies-spike-10-year-highs

Durden, T. (2017, August 7). US Credit Card Debt Surpasses Financial Crisis Record, As Student And Auto Loans Hit New All Time High. Retrieved from https://www.zerohedge.com/news/2017-08-07/us-credit-card-debt-surpasses-financial-crisis-record-student-and-auto-loans-hit-new

Durden, T. (2017, December 04). Stock Market 2018: The Tao Vs. Central Banks. Retrieved from http://www.zerohedge.com/news/2017-12-04/stock-market-2018-tao-vs-central-banks

Durden, T. (2017, December 04). "For The First Time In Modern History" US Government Debt Will Surpass Household Debt. Retrieved from http://www.zerohedge.com/news/2017-12-04/first-time-modern-history-us-government-debt-will-surpass-household-debt

Durden, T. (2017, December 07). Finally, An Honest Inflation Index - Guess What It Shows. Retrieved from http://www.zerohedge.com/news/2017-12-07/ finally-honest-inflation-index-guess-what-it-shows

Durden, T. (2017, December 07). Record Calm Stock Market Gets A Shock. Retrieved from https://www.zerohedge.com/news/2017-12-07/record-calm-stock-market-gets-shock

Durden, T. (2017, December 07). Why The Globalists Need A War... And Soon. Retrieved from https://www.zerohedge.com/news/2017-12-07/why-globalists-need-war-and-soon

Durden, T. (2017, December 11). Deutsche: "We Are Almost At The Point Beyond Which There Will Be No More Bubbles". Retrieved from https://www. zerohedge.com/news/2017-12-11/deutsche-we-are-almost-point-beyond-which-there-will-be-no-more-bubbles

Durden, T. (2017, December 11). Doug Noland: There Will Be No Way Out When This Market Bubble Bursts. Retrieved from https://www.zerohedge. com/news/2017-12-11/doug-noland-there-will-be-no-way-out-when-market-bubble-bursts

Durden, T. (2017, December 13). Gundlach Reveals His Favorite Trade For 2018. Retrieved from https://www.zerohedge.com/news/2017-12-13/gund-lach-reveals-his-favorite-trade-2018

Durden, T. (2017, December 13). Jamie Dimon Says Corporations Will Fund Buybacks With Tax Cuts And That's "Not A Bad Thing". Retrieved from https://www.zerohedge.com/news/2017-12-13/jamie-dimon-says-corpora-tions-will-fund-buybacks-tax-cuts-and-thats-not-bad-thing

Durden, T. (2017, December 13). Liesman Asks Yellen: "Is The Fed Worried By The Market Going Up Triple Digits Every Day?" Retrieved from https:// www.zerohedge.com/news/2017-12-13/yellen-bitcoin-highly-speculative-as-set-record-high-stocks-are-not-flashing-red-or-e

Durden, T. (2017, December 18). Taxphoria Sparks Stock-Buying Panic - Dow Does Something It Has Never Ever Done Before. Retrieved from https:// www.zerohedge.com/news/2017-12-18/taxphoria-sparks-stock-buying-pan-ic-dow-does-something-it-has-never-ever-done

Durden, T. (2017, December 19). 2018: Irrational Complacency - "What Is Your Exit Strategy?" Retrieved from https://www.zerohedge.com/ news/2017-12-19/2018-irrational-complacency-what-your-exit-strategy

Durden, T. (2017, December 22). Sharing Risks To Counter Germany's Plans Seeing Target2 Collaterilazation With Gold Reserves. Retrieved from https://www.zerohedge.com/news/2017-12-21/sharing-risks-counter-germanys-plans-seeing-target2-collaterilazation-gold-reserves

Durden, T. (2017, December 30). The Greatest Bubble Ever: Why You Better Believe It - Part 2. Retrieved from https://www.zerohedge.com/news/2017-12-29/greatest-bubble-ever-why-you-better-believe-it-part-2

Durden, T. (2017, December 30). The Greatest Bubble Ever: Why You Better Believe It - Part 2. Retrieved from https://www.zerohedge.com/news/2017-12-29/greatest-bubble-ever-why-you-better-believe-it-part-2

Durden, T. (2017, July 21). "May The Bursting Of The Student Loan Bubble Commence!" Retrieved from https://www.zerohedge.com/news/2017-07-21/may-bursting-student-loan-bubble-commence

Durden, T. (2017, June 20). Good Luck Getting Out Of That Subprime Auto Loan When Used Car Prices Crash. Retrieved from https://www.zerohedge.com/news/2017-06-19/good-luck-getting-out-subprime-auto-loan-when-used-car-prices-crash

Durden, T. (2017, March 22). This New Bubble Is Even Bigger Than The Subprime Fiasco. Retrieved from https://www.zerohedge.com/news/2017-03-22/new-bubble-even-bigger-subprime-fiasco

Durden, T. (2017, November 14). The Fed Issues A Subprime Warning As Household Debt Hits A New All Time High. Retrieved from https://www.zerohedge.com/news/2017-11-14/fed-issues-subprime-warning-household-debt-hits-new-all-time-high

Durden, T. (2017, November 14). The Fed Issues A Subprime Warning As Household Debt Hits A New All Time High. Retrieved from https://www.zerohedge.com/news/2017-11-14/fed-issues-subprime-warning-household-debt-hits-new-all-time-high

Durden, T. (2017, November 15). Looking For Inflation In All The Wrong Places. Retrieved from https://www.zerohedge.com/news/2017-11-15/looking-inflation-all-wrong-places

Durden, T. (2017, November 16). Rickards On Gold, Interest Rates, & Super-Cycles. Retrieved from https://www.zerohedge.com/news/2017-11-16/rickards-gold-interest-rates-super-cycles

Durden, T. (2017, November 17). Bill Blain: "Stock Markets Don't Matter; The Great Crash Of 2018 Will Start In The Bond Market". Retrieved from https://www.zerohedge.com/news/2017-11-17/bill-blain-stock-markets-dont-matter-great-crash-2018-will-start-bond-market

Durden, T. (2017, November 18). Golden Catalysts. Retrieved from https://www.zerohedge.com/news/2017-11-18/golden-catalysts

Durden, T. (2017, November 18). Is America In Terminal Decline? Retrieved from https://www.zerohedge.com/news/2017-11-18/america-terminal-decline

Durden, T. (2017, November 18). The Great Retirement Con. Retrieved from https://www.zerohedge.com/news/2017-11-18/great-retirement-con

Durden, T. (2017, November 19). A Fiscal Disappointment - Of Tax Reform & Growth Fairies. Retrieved from https://www.zerohedge.com/news/2017-11-19/fiscal-disappointment-tax-reform-growth-fairies

Durden, T. (2017, November 19). The Difference Between GAAP And Non-GAAP Q3 EPS For The Dow Jones Was 16%. Retrieved from https://www.zerohedge.com/news/2017-11-19/difference-between-gaap-and-non-gaap-q3-eps-dow-jones-was-16

Durden, T. (2017, November 19). The Stage Has Been Set For The Next Financial Crisis. Retrieved from https://www.zerohedge.com/news/2017-11-19/stage-has-been-set-next-financial-crisis

Durden, T. (2017, November 20). Bubble Dynamics and Market Crashes. Retrieved from https://www.zerohedge.com/news/2017-11-20/bubble-dynamics-and-market-crashes

Durden, T. (2017, November 20). Gold Versus Bitcoin: The Pro-Gold Argument Takes Shape. Retrieved from https://www.zerohedge.com/news/2017-11-20/gold-versus-bitcoin-pro-gold-argument-takes-shape

Durden, T. (2017, November 22). 11 Charts Exposing The Madness Of The Stock Market Crowd. Retrieved from https://www.zerohedge.com/news/2017-11-22/11-charts-exposing-madness-stock-market-crowd

Durden, T. (2017, November 7). About 33% Of Students Drop Out Of College; Here's How Many Go On To Default On Their Student Debt. Retrieved from https://www.zerohedge.com/news/2017-11-06/about-33-students-drop-out-college-heres-how-many-go-default-their-student-debt

Durden, T. (2017, November 7). The World's Biggest Bubbles. Retrieved from https://www.zerohedge.com/news/2017-11-07/worlds-largest-bubbles-ranked-algebris-investments

Durden, T. (2017, November 7). US Credit Card Debt Rises Above $1 Trillion As Student, Auto Loans Hit All Time High. Retrieved from https://www.zerohedge.com/news/2017-11-07/us-credit-card-debt-rises-above-1-trillion-student-auto-loans-hit-all-time-high

Durden, T. (2017, September 18). Pension Storm Coming: "This Will Become One Of The Most Heated Battles Of My Lifetime". Retrieved from https://www.zerohedge.com/news/2017-09-17/pension-storm-coming-will-become-one-most-heated-battles-my-lifetime

Durden, T. (2017, September 28). Is The Bubble About To Burst? Student-Loan Delinquency Rates Rise For First Time In Years. Retrieved from https://www.zerohedge.com/news/2017-09-28/bubble-about-burst-student-loan-delinquency-rates-rise-first-time-years

Durden, T. (2018, January 07). Global Debt Hits Record $233 Trillion, Up $16Tn In 9 Months. Retrieved from https://www.zerohedge.com/news/2018-01-07/global-debt-hits-record-233-trillion-16-trillion-9-months

Durden, T. (2018, January 22). "We Can't Pretend Interest Payments Aren't Rising Anymore..." Retrieved from https://www.zerohedge.com/news/2018-01-22/we-cant-pretend-interest-payments-arent-rising-anymore

Durden, T. (2018, January 26). Investor Cash Just Hit An All Time Low. Retrieved from https://www.zerohedge.com/news/2018-01-26/investor-cash-just-hit-all-time-low

Durden, T. (2018, January 28). "Investors Are Residing In A Surreal World", But One Banker Thinks It's All About To Change. Retrieved from https://www.zerohedge.com/news/2018-01-28/investors-are-residing-surreal-world-one-banker-thinks-its-all-about-change

Durden, T. (2018, January 29). Bonds Finally Noticed What Is Going On... Stocks Are Next. Retrieved from https://www.zerohedge.com/news/2018-01-28/bonds-finally-noticed-what-going-stocks-are-next

Durden, T. (2018, March 15). It's Just Starting: Moody's Warns A Deluge Of Retail Bankruptcies Is Coming. Retrieved from https://www.zerohedge.com/news/2018-03-15/its-just-starting-moodys-warns-deluge-retail-bankruptcies-coming

Durden, T. (n.d.). How The Fed Destroyed The Functioning American Democracy And Bankrupted The Nation. Retrieved from https://www.zerohedge.com/news/2017-11-13/how-fed-destroyed-functioning-american-democracy-and-bankrupted-nation

Edwards, J. (2017, August 06). What Mark Carney knows but dare not say out loud. Retrieved from http://www.businessinsider.com/uk-savings-rate-consumer-debt-mark-carney-bank-of-england-2017-8?r=UK&IR=T

Federal Reserve Economic Data | FRED | St. Louis Fed. (n.d.). Retrieved from https://fred.stlouisfed.org/

Frum, D. (2014, December 24). The Real Story of How America Became an Economic Superpower. Retrieved from https://www.theatlantic.com/international/archive/2014/12/the-real-story-of-how-america-became-an-economic-superpower/384034/

G. (2018, February 08). Peak Gold: Global Gold Supply Flat In 2017 As China Output Falls By 9%. Retrieved from https://www.zerohedge.com/news/2018-02-08/peak-gold-global-gold-supply-flat-2017-china-output-falls-9

Geiger, A. (2017, August 23). U.S. edge on favorability around the world shrinks. Retrieved from http://www.pewresearch.org/fact-tank/2017/08/23/in-global-popularity-contest-u-s-and-china-not-russia-vie-for-first/ft_17-08-11_china_us_russia_trend/

Grant Williams. (n.d.). Retrieved from https://stansberrystreaming.com/presentations/grant-williams.html

Hansen, W. (2017, August 03). Understanding the Fractional Reserve Banking System. Retrieved from https://www.learningmarkets.com/understanding-the-fractional-reserve-banking-system/

Holodny, E. (2015, September 18). The 5,000-year history of interest rates shows just how historically low US rates are right now. Retrieved from http://www.businessinsider.com/chart-5000-years-of-interest-rates-2015-9

Johnston, M. (2015, December 22). Bretton Woods: How It Changed the World. Retrieved from https://www.investopedia.com/articles/forex/122215/bretton-woods-system-how-it-changed-world.asp

Kratimenos, M. (2002). Aurum metallicum (2002). Retrieved from https://www.britishhomeopathic.org/charity/how-we-can-help/articles/homeopathic-medicines/a/the-golden-cure/

Maher, B. (2017, November 21). What the "Yield Curve" Predicts for the Economy. Retrieved from https://dailyreckoning.com/yield-curve-predicts-economy/

Mandatory and Discretionary Spending. (2018, February 14). Retrieved from https://www.pgpf.org/chart-archive/0185_dual_crowdout

Mandatory Spending Composition. (2017, August 15). Retrieved from https://www.pgpf.org/Chart-Archive/0191_mandatory_spending

Mandatory Spending Is Growing over Time. (2018, March 22). Retrieved from https://www.pgpf.org/chart-archive/0156_mandatory_discretionary_pies

Marks, H. (2018, January 23). Latest memo from Howard Marks: Latest Thinking. Retrieved from https://www.oaktreecapital.com/insights/howard-marks-memos

Mauldin, J. (2017, December 06). Opinion: There's overwhelming evidence that the U.S. stock market is heading for disaster. Retrieved from https://www.marketwatch.com/story/theres-overwhelming-evidence-that-the-us-stock-market-is-heading-for-disaster-2017-12-05/print

Mauldin, J. (2017, May 22). The Great Reset: How Should We Then Invest? Retrieved from https://www.mauldineconomics.com/frontlinethoughts/the-great-reset-how-should-we-then-invest

Maverick, J. (2015, November 04). Why Does the House Always Win? A Look at Casino Profitability. Retrieved from https://www.investopedia.com/articles/personal-finance/110415/why-does-house-always-win-look-casino-profitability.asp

Meisler, L. (2017, June 30). Pension Fund Problems Worsen in 43 States. Retrieved from https://www.bloomberg.com/graphics/2017-state-pension-funding-ratios/

Meisler, L. (2017, June 30). Pension Fund Problems Worsen in 43 States. Retrieved from https://www.bloomberg.com/graphics/2017-state-pension-funding-ratios/

Miller, D. (2018, January 19). Can Americans Really Depend on Social Security? Retrieved from https://www.equities.com/news/can-americans-really-depend-on-social-security

Nasiripour, S., & Forster, N. (2017, March 23). 3 Charts That Show Just How Dire The Student Debt Crisis Has Become. Retrieved from https://www.huffingtonpost.com/entry/3-charts-student-debt-crisis_us_56b0e9d0e-4b0a1b96203d369

Nike. YouTube, YouTube, 16 July 2007, www.youtube.com/watch?v=qLEC-MCargd8.

Pattison, D. (2015, February 01). Social Security Administration. Retrieved from https://www.ssa.gov/policy/docs/ssb/v75n1/v75n1p1.html

Periodic Table with Names of Elements. (2015, November 08). Retrieved from https://sciencenotes.org/periodic-table-with-names-of-elements/

Rappaport, J., & Redmond, M. (2016). Consumer-price inflation and inflation targets. Retrieved from https://www.kansascityfed.org/publications/research/mb/articles/2016/consumer-price-inflations-rising-rent-west.

REPORTS. (n.d.). Retrieved from https://www.treasurydirect.gov/govt/reports/ir/ir_expense.htm

Roach, S. S. (2016, February 18). Central Banking Goes Negative by Stephen S. Roach. Retrieved from https://www.project-syndicate.org/commentary/central-banks-negative-interest-rates-by-stephen-s--roach-2016-02

Roser, M., & Ortiz-Ospina, E. (2014). World Population Growth. Retrieved from https://ourworldindata.org/world-population-growth

S. (2018, January 21). Chinese Physical Gold Investment Demand Surges While Americans Pile Into Stock & Crypto Bubbles. Retrieved from https://www.zerohedge.com/news/2018-01-21/chinese-physical-gold-investment-demand-surges-while-americans-pile-stock-crypto

Scorsese, Martin, Winkler, Irwin, and Nicholas Pileggi. Goodfellas. Warner Brothers, 1990.

Shatz, H. (2017, November 06). The Long-Term Budget Shortfall and National Security: A Problem the United States Should Stop Avoiding. Retrieved from https://warontherocks.com/2017/11/the-long-term-budget-shortfall-and-national-security-a-problem-the-united-states-should-stop-avoiding/

Sorry to burst your bubble. (2015, July 16). Retrieved from https://www.economist.com/news/finance-and-economics/21657817-new-research-suggests-it-debt-not-frothy-asset-prices-should-worry

Staff, I. (2018, April 28). Capital Flows. Retrieved from https://www.investo-pedia.com/terms/c/capital-flows.asp

Stein, D. J. (1932). Gold in History and in Modern Times. Retrieved from http://www.thepresentage.net/wp-content/uploads/Gold-in-History-and-in-Modern-Times.pdf

Stockman, D. (2017, November 21). The Illusion of Growth. Retrieved from https://dailyreckoning.com/the-illusion-of-growth/

SuggestedByYou. YouTube, YouTube, 15 May 2015, www.youtube.com/watch?v=ZEIkcMJLZI0.

Sykes, C. J. (2017, November 17). Charles J. Sykes: What happened to the party of fiscal responsibility? Retrieved from https://www.ohio.com/akron/editorial/commentary/charles-j-sykes-what-happened-to-the-party-of-fiscal-responsibility

The wit and wisdom of Warren Buffett. (n.d.). Retrieved from http://fortune.com/2012/11/19/the-wit-and-wisdom-of-warren-buffett/

Top 10 Things You Didn't Know About Money. (2009, August 05). Retrieved from http://content.time.com/time/specials/packages/article/0,28804,1914560_1914558_1914593,00.html

Townsend, M., Surane, J., Orr, E., & Cannon, C. (2017, November 08). America's 'Retail Apocalypse' Is Really Just Beginning. Retrieved from https://www.bloomberg.com/graphics/2017-retail-debt/

Tully, S. (2017, September 22). America Will Soon Face a $1 Trillion Budget Deficit. Do Voters Care? Retrieved from http://fortune.com/2017/09/22/united-states-budget-deficit/

U.S. Immigration History | U.S. Immigration Policy - Environmental Impact Statement |. (n.d.). Retrieved from http://www.immigrationeis.org/about-ieis/us-immigration-history

Udland, M. (2016, January 04). The incredible rise of the $4 trillion equity index fund business in 1 chart. Retrieved from http://www.businessinsider.com/index-fund-assets-under-management-2016-1

Umoh, R. (2017, September 22). Billionaire Warren Buffett could win $2 million thanks to a bet he made 10 years ago. Retrieved from https://www.cnbc.com/2017/09/18/warren-buffett-won-2-million-from-a-bet-that-he-made-ten-years-ago.html

United States one hundred-dollar bill. (2017, November 20). Retrieved from https://en.wikipedia.org/wiki/United_States_one_hundred-dollar_bill

US & World Debt Visualized in 100 Dollar Bills. (2014, January 01). Retrieved from http://rockstone-research.com/index.php/en/news/554-US-&-World-Debt-Visualized-in-100-Dollar-Bills

US & World Debt Visualized in 100 Dollar Bills. (n.d.). Retrieved from http://rockstone-research.com/index.php/en/news/554-US-&-World-Debt-Visualized-in-100-Dollar-Bills

Vaidyanath, R. (2017, August 24). US Corporate Bonds Hitting a Peak? Retrieved from https://www.theepochtimes.com/us-corporate-bonds-hitting-a-peak_2285626.html

Watts, W. (2017, October 28). Why stock-market bulls should be wary of rising tide of earnings shenanigans. Retrieved from https://www.marketwatch.com/story/why-stock-market-bulls-should-be-wary-of-rising-tide-of-earnings-shenanigans-2017-10-28

Williams-Grut, O. (2016, December 07). Mark Carney's 'lost decade' in one stark chart. Retrieved from http://www.businessinsider.com/mark-carneys-lost-decade-chart-collapse-real-wage-growth-bank-of-england-2016-12

Morgan James
Speakers Group

We connect Morgan James published authors with live and online events and audiences who will benefit from their expertise.

Morgan James makes all of our titles available through the Library for All Charity Organization.

www.LibraryForAll.org

CPSIA information can be obtained
at www.ICGtesting.com
Printed in the USA
BVHW07*1224260618
519754BV00001B/1/P

9 781642 791068